Adolphus William Ward

The House of Austria in The Thirty Years´ War

Salzwasser

Adolphus William Ward

The House of Austria in The Thirty Years´ War

1. Auflage | ISBN: 978-3-84605-572-4

Erscheinungsort: Frankfurt, Deutschland

Erscheinungsjahr: 2020

Salzwasser Verlag GmbH

Reprint of the original, first published in 1869.

THE HOUSE OF AUSTRIA

IN

THE THIRTY YEARS' WAR.

LECTURE I.

IT is well that princes should read history; but it is not well that history should be written for them by their servants. In the century and the country of the Thirty Years' War, the historical author, even if his identity was not lost among the crowd of menial existences of the courts, well knew for what and for whom he plied his pen. Even to those whose own tastes or beliefs induced them to contribute their aid towards collecting or confusing the memorials of the times, there seemed to have been given, together with their semi-official task, a semi-official conscience,—which conducted their blindfold march along a tortuous path, but to no doubtful goal. As a result they have left to posterity much, which (in Bolingbroke's phrase) it may neglect entirely, not only without detriment, but with advantage. Since those days of abasement, great and salutary changes have supervened. Even before the German

B

nation had resolved to break with the traditions
of its dynasties, both great and small, a spirit of
freedom had begun to stir the dry leaves on which
were written the records of its humiliations. The
revival of a nation casts its wholesome rays behind
as well as before it ; yet in historical literature, as
in political life, the Germany of the present has
not wholly emerged out of a period of transition.
Dynastic history is still cultivated in more than
one capital whence dynastic government has taken
its unwilling departure. In the South, historical
questions are still occasionally treated in a spirit
of Tyrolese devotion. In the victorious North,
Heaven is still believed to be on the side of a
particular house; and the imperfect satisfaction of
a nation's hopes is registered as only another page
in the consistent memoirs of a watchful line. But
the times are sore for the over-trustful and the
over-credulous; new historical fallacies are only
compounded with the result of exploding the mould
of the fabricator, while the old are expiring with a
last feeble hiss. For, happily, the vitality which
credulity bestows is not everlasting. The wisdom
of dynasties must justify itself from their own
archives; and as the doors of these treasuries are
opened, and the serene light of scientific inquiry
streams in over their dust, the epoch is at hand

when dynastic history, like dynastic statecraft, will be a thing of the past.

It is not as an offering of homage to the House of Austria, that the coming historian of the Thirty Years' War, be he living or yet unborn, will bestow upon the world a long-desired gift. It is no new Annals of the Ferdinands, neither is it any new jeremiad against the treason of the Protestant princes, and the self-seeking avarice of their allies, which will satisfy the awakened historic sense of these latter days. Soon there will hardly remain an Austrian university whose students will tolerate the reappearance of the House of Habsburg in the favourite character of victim to a European conspiracy. On the other hand, the unscrupulous opponents of that house have long been defended past all prospect of rehabilitation. Even the view formerly current as to the motives and conduct of the great Swedish invader is in these days chiefly left to stray patriots from Stockholm, hopeful of haranguing a North-German audience into the conviction that King William, the protector of Luther's statue at Worms, has assumed the inheritance of Dugald Dalgetty's Lion of the North.[1] The history of the Thirty Years' War can no longer be written, as if each successive book were but one

[1] See Notes at end of Lectures.

more lunge in the duel between religious prejudices or national antipathies; and, least of all, can the interests of the House of Austria, which has registered the opening of a new era in its annals, require the historian to go forth like Wallenstein to the battle of Lützen, trusting in his impenetrability.

In the observations which I shall have the honour of submitting to your consideration on this and a future night, I must necessarily restrict myself to certain aspects of a very wide and complicated subject. The policy and conduct of the House of Austria in a war which its chief hero, Gustavus Adolphus, declared to have absorbed into itself all the other wars of Europe,([2]) involve in their sphere questions at which my limits forbid me even to glance, but which even the most summary historical narrative could not afford to overlook. If, therefore, in my remarks to-night concerning the genesis of that policy, and on a subsequent occasion concerning its development, I should frequently seem liable to the charge of omissions, I am at all events aware of the danger which attends any rapid survey of such a subject as this; and I can only plead the absence of any intention on my part to imitate certain writers on the same subject, who have found in it frequent opportunities of being brief, because it was their design to be obscure.

The half century of anarchy known as the reign of Frederick III. had witnessed the collapse of the Imperial, and the revival of the Papal power; but amidst its disappointments and humiliations it had been unable to lay the spirit of a national longing for reform in Church and State.(³)　Before the close of the fifteenth century, Maximilian I. sat in his father's seat, strong in the possession of the compactest territory united under the dominion of any German prince, and buoyed up by the prospect of acquisitions which would enable the House of Habsburg to hold its own among the great dynasties of Europe.　From him, a German in everything but heart and soul, the nation had hoped for the willing accomplishment of the task which his predecessor had renounced with cynical apathy.(⁴)　But instead of regenerating the Empire by a genuine revision of its administrative system, Maximilian I. bent his thoughts upon establishing beyond its borders the influence of his house; instead of becoming the second founder of German unity, he merely became the father of an institution which his people could have well spared, that of the mercenaries of the lowlands— the *Landsknechte.*　He valued the Imperial crown which he laboured so hard to secure to his grand-son Charles; for to the Imperial position of

his father and himself his house owed those
marrriages through which it was to achieve its
European predominance. But though he would
not resign a single Imperial privilege which he regarded as other than illusory, he was found ready
to sacrifice a German province in order to obtain
two Eastern matrimonial alliances ; and at his
last Diet, when the Estates were demanding the
redress of their ecclesiastical grievances, was significantly supported by a Papal legate, in his
endeavour to obtain a general levy for a crusade
against the Turks—Turks in Italy, said the Ger-
mans. When Maximilian I. closed his chivalrous
career—for was he not, is he not almost to this
day, in poetry and prose, saluted as the "Last
German Knight," while in truth he ought to be
remembered as the first German *Landsknecht ?*—
he had virtually assured to his grandson Charles
the Imperial dignity which was henceforth to be
degraded into an appanage of the House of Habsburg. True, he had successively offered his aid
for securing the same dignity to King Lewis the
Jagellone, and to the juvenile and credulous ambition of the English Henry VIII. But their
hopes speedily vanished on the death of the Emperor, whom Frederick the Wise of Saxony called
"the politest of men ;" the money of Francis of

France was scattered in vain; and in June 1519, a Spanish Habsburg wore, in addition to eleven other crowns, that of the Empire. "Dutch and Welsh," sings a jubilant ballad of the day, "are in his power; though few are the years of this young Archduke of Austria."

To Charles V. the nation came to owe—besides a system of military armaments, which, wonderful to relate, survived the Seven Years' War, and lasted till the dissolution of the Empire in the days of Napoleon (⁵)—its permanent disintegration. That Charles should have accepted the Reformation of Luther, in the sense in which it was accepted by the Elector of Saxony, would have been for him to renounce a religious belief to which, as there is every reason to conclude, he from first to last conscientiously adhered. That, when it was in every sense a national movement, and before it bore the hateful name of Lutheran, the self-assured name of Evangelical, the ominous name of Protestant, he should have met it by concessions such as the conjuncture demanded from a national sovereign, would have been for him to have lost less than he was in the end forced to sacrifice; and to have preserved the unity of the nation. It was not Rome which drove him to the attitude which he assumed, but the use which he

desired to make of Rome.   An emperor who held
in his hands a power never compassed by any of
the successors of Charlemagne, had entered into
a conflict with the spirit of the German nation.
Thus he enabled the princes who were individually
impotent against him to identify the unsolidation
of their territorial autonomy with the national
cause ; and, as a distinguished modern historian
has so well said, (⁶) by his endeavour to restore
Catholicism according to the Spanish pattern,
Charles V. convinced all Europe that the same
fate menaced it which he had prepared for his
own Pyrenean peninsula.

The Reformation, unhappily not without the
aid of treason and corruption, had not only
worsted Charles in the great conflict to which
he had challenged it in the fulness of his power,
it had literally driven him from the Imperial
throne.   The struggle had, to adapt another expression of the same writer, been one against a
dynastic ambition desirous of reviving the Teu-
tonic dream of the Middle Ages by the methods
of Italian statecraft.   Spain and Italy had sug-
gested the means for restoring the universal
monarchy, in which the successor of Charlemagne
was to be the temporal viceregent of God on
earth.   But the struggle against this design had,

in its turn, been carried on in the interests of lesser dynastic ambitions, to which "German liberty" was a technical expression (*Deutsche Libertät*), and religious liberty a thing unknown—ambitions, moreover, willing to sacrifice the integrity of the Empire to the attainment of their individual ends. The Treaty of Passau, and the Peace of Augsburg (for which the former paved the way), established the victory of the Protestant cause within certain limits; but this cause could no longer be called that of the nation, when its triumph had been purchased by the loss of three German territories. The French king had, for the first time, crossed the frontier as *vindex libertatis Germanicæ;* and though his German allies were eager to withdraw from the shameful league, France clung to the prize which she had cheaply secured—clung to it, till a century afterwards it was legally incorporated in the French monarchy in the Peace of Westphalia.(7) And thus Germany, which to the dynastic ambition of the greatest of the Habsburgs owed the perpetuation of her weakness, saw the greed and the terror of his opponents begin a new page in her history—the most shameful which its records contain. France henceforth had a footing in the Empire; nor has she ever since awoke from the hallucination that a

river German on either bank, from source to sea,
was designed by nature—for it is nature who is
credited with the device—as a boundary-line.

While in Spain Charles V.'s son and successor,
with dull but deadly obstinacy, pursued the ideal
of his father's reign,—the establishment of a universal monarchy, where the ruler should be at
once the protector and the secular director of the
Universal Church,—the Austrian branch of the
House of Habsburg entered upon an interval of
compromise. The family compact which had
been intended to secure a close co-operation
between the two branches, by identifying their interests, was a thing of the past; and the Austrian
branch was left, as best it might, to confront its
own difficulties and dangers. Not that Ferdinand I.
was without his projects for the advance of his
branch of the dynasty. He would have pressed
a project of marrying one of his sons to Queen
Mary of England, had he not learnt that his
brother (whose word was law) had destined this
combination for his son Philip. But Ferdinand
was one of those sovereigns whom the House of
Austria seems privileged from time to time to
produce, who display a striking facility for per-
ceiving the error of their ways, and of the ways
of their predecessors. The collapse of the policy

of Charles V. seems to have convinced his brother
of the impossibility of staying the progress of
Protestantism, at all events for the present; nor
were his later relations to Rome such as to
animate his desire to resist the inroads of heresy.
The Peace of Augsburg of the year 1555, the
basis on which the Empire was preserved from
the outbreak of more than transitory hostilities
till the commencement of the Thirty Years' War,
contained a critical clause. This was the so-called
Reservatum Ecclesiasticum, which the Protestants
refused to acknowledge as an integral part of
the entire instrument. (8) Yet, even so, Pope
Paul IV. had made the non-observance of the
treaty a condition of his recognition of Ferdinand I.
as emperor; and though he was actually acknowledged by Pope Pius IV., yet the latter only
looked upon the treaty as a temporary arrangement awaiting violation at the first convenient
opportunity. The Jesuit "opinion" which this
pontiff's successor, Pius V., obtained, to the effect
that the clauses of the treaty were not legal
ordinances, but mere *de facto* statements as to
the present, which the future might alter, left a
significant opening for sovereigns whose necessity
for a pacific policy might be less than that of
Ferdinand I. But during his reign, it was Pro-

testantism which found itself able to enact the
part of the aggressor. It invaded the territories
of the House of Austria, and, though Ferdinand
had authorized the promulgation of the decrees
of the Council of Trent in the Empire, besides
entering into a general undertaking to resist
heresy, in order to conciliate the Papal acquiescence in his tenure of the Imperial throne, he
contrived to play fast and loose with the privileges
conceded by him to his Protestant subjects, without giving violent umbrage to either side. Thus
he steered the crazy vessel, without foundering it
upon the rocks which beset his course, till the
day of his death in 1564.

Before he died, he had divided the possessions
of the German Habsburgs among his three sons;
like Lewis the Pious, breaking up the inheritance
of Charlemagne. Austria proper fell to Maximilian, who succeeded his father as Emperor, and
as King of Bohemia and of Hungary; the Tyrol
to Archduke Ferdinand; and Styria with Carinthia
and Carniola to Archduke Charles. (Thus we
have for a time to distinguish between three
German lines; but the Tyrolese expired with its
founder, whose marriage with the fair Philippina
Welser, famed in German story, left him without
heirs capable of succeeding to his dominions.)

The Emperor Maximilian II. was regarded as a
Protestant at heart; and it was with difficulty that
he obtained the Papal recognition. In considering
the reign of this amiable prince from the point of
view under which I am endeavouring to trace the
policy of his house in its bearing upon the outbreak of the Great War, it is hard to deny that
his virtues and his weaknesses combined to ripen
the situation for that outbreak. Maximilian II.
had, as it seems to me, received into his inmost
heart Melanchthon's lessons of tolerance; and who
can fail to sympathise with that most attractive
of historical spectacles—a mind in advance of its
times? If, in order to secure the Imperial crown,
Maximilian II. allowed himself to be argued into
a good son of the Church, it was not, like
Henry the Bearnese, in pure gaiety of heart
that he changed his convictions. Like the lover
of Gabrielle, Maximilian may in his youth have
cared more for the fair ladies than for the theo-
logians who adorned his table; but it is obvious
from a survey of his system of government when
he came to the throne, that in him toleration was
not, as in Henry IV. of France, the result of a
mixture of *bonhomie* and indifference.(⁹) Maximilian's method of governing with a loose rein
would have allowed the whole of his hereditary

dominions to be gradually Lutheranised, had it
not been for the marvellous exertions of the
Jesuits, who here established one of their strongest
claims upon the gratitude of Rome. As it was,
in Austria and Styria the Protestant lords were
allowed the free exercise of their religion; and,
with the aid of pastors from Wittenberg, fast converted their tenantry; while in Bohemia religious
liberty was virtually permitted; Silesia and Moravia as usual sharing the fortunes of the sister-
dominion. Yet it was not toleration by an
individual sovereign, but a legally-defined position,
independent of the individuality of himself or
his successors, which Maximilian, warned by his
knowledge of the character of his probable successor, should have bestowed upon Protestantism,
if he was really minded to open a new era for his
states. A charter such as the Bohemians afterwards extorted from Rhodolph might, if granted
by Maximilian, have founded religious liberty upon
a basis which even the determination of Ferdinand II. would have proved unable to shake; while
the *permanent* establishment of the privileges of
the Austrian and Styrian Estates would have
proved an obstacle to the same prince in the first
step which he took towards the great reaction.
And meanwhile, though at home his policy was

liberal, abroad Maximilian II. was entirely de-
pendent upon the guidance of his brother-in-law
the Spanish Philip ; and while he ensured himself
popularity at home by his toleration towards his
Protestant subjects, he never availed himself of
this popularity to free his government from its
humiliating position of a tributary to the arch
enemy of Christianity, the Turk.

The necessities of Ferdinand I. and the weakness of Maximilian II. had reduced the dynastic
power of the House of Austria to a benevolent
dignity. Neither at home nor abroad could their
policy be said to amount even to what previous
emperors had been content to secure as the essence
of government—*police.* ([10]) The whole of Austria,
and nearly the whole of Styria and its sister-
duchies, were mainly Lutheran ; Bohemia, Silesia,
and Moravia were fermenting with every form of
Christian belief ; and Catholicism had all been but
driven back into the mountains of the Tyrol—when
in 1576 a fanatical, a Spanish Catholic, ascended
the Imperial throne, as well as those of Bohemia
and Hungary, in the person of Rhodolph II.

The fatal cycle was now almost complete ; for
Rhodolph II. was one of those princes who, like
Louis XV. of France, seem passive instruments in
the hands of the evil genius of their people.   The

dilemma of the situation must soon prove un-
avoidable. And, whether the religious policy which
Ferdinand I. had found himself constrained by
necessity to adopt, and to which Maximilian II.
had been inclined by his early associations and by
his natural disposition, was to be allowed to run
its course; or whether the Austrian branch of the
House of Habsburg was, in the conduct of religious
matters, as well as of foreign affairs, to join hands
with the Spanish monarch: the management of
the situation required a strong will, a steady hand,
and an unflagging energy. No longer untouched
by the national heresy, but filled in their length
and breadth with Lutheran lords, and burghers, and
peasants, the hereditary dominions of the House
must be forced to return into the lines of the
orthodox faith, or be for ever freed from its
claim to an undivided sway. No longer supine in
indifference, the Pontiff was ready to. sanction his
Spanish champion's use of fire and sword for the
suppression of the abomination of heresy; the
Council of Trent had pronounced the *ultimatum*
of the Church; the Order of Jesus was at work
in the front of an unprecedented Catholic reaction; and the Inquisition was on the watch to
extend the sphere of its tremendous operations.
No longer surrounded by feeble neighbours, but

threatened by the growth of vigorous monarchies
in north and north-east,—with the ancient arch-
enemy knocking loudly at the south-eastern gate,
already half opened for his entrance,—and with
France emerging from *her* thirty years' war as
the most dangerous, because the best-consolidated
monarchy of Europe, intimately allied with her
victorious neighbours across the narrow seas and
her north-eastern borders ; the Empire in the course
of Rhodolph's reign seemed marked out as the
prey of foreign ambition, unless (whether in alliance
with Spain or not) a strong hand at the helm could
give it unity at all events against the stranger.

Such were some, and some only, of the difficulties
which beset this reign ; and what was the character
of the sovereign who was called upon to meet them,
and the character of his government ? Of Rhodolph II. we possess portraits in the two periods
of his life which an Austrian historian,*([11]) whose
labours on the transaction of this reign have thrown
a totally new light upon many of its conjunctures,
has characterised as the "phlegmatic" and the
"melancholy." But Rhodolph's phlegm amounted
to apathy, and his melancholy passed the bounds
of mania. And it was his peculiar and perhaps
unparalleled fate, to be forced into taking an active

* Gindely.

C

part in the direction or disturbance of affairs when his mania had become uncontrollable, and when years had developed in him that last resource of the impotent—obstinacy. By education he was a Spaniard; for, during the childhood of the wretched epileptic Don Carlos, Philip, uncertain as to the life of this his sole heir, had been fain to bring up the Archduke and his brother Ernest at his own court as possible successors to his thrones. The influences of a court which, in the opinion of Catherine de Medici, transformed even her daughter, a Medici and a Valois, into a thorough Spaniard, and which actually thus transformed a son of William of Orange—had deepened the natural gloom of a mind in which, as in that of more than one other Habsburg, rankled the fatal heritage of the mad Joanna. When in his twenty-fifth year Rhodolph ascended his thrones, he brought with him the manners and sentiments, but not the indefatigable energy of the Spanish king ; nor the belief in himself which, notwithstanding the philippics of distinguished historians, saves the royal scribe of the Escurial from the contempt of posterity. Like Philip, Rhodolph was rarely known to smile ; and his favourite companion was solitude. From the first he shut himself up at Prague in his cabinet of curiosities, among his astronomical instruments and mechanical toys

avoiding royal sports and exercises, first as much
as possible, and then altogether. Like Charles V.
he had a love of horses ; but he soon came to
content himself with domiciliary visits to his costly
stud. Like Philip II. he was not without a tendency to secret debauchery, and loved, sultan-
wise, to sin in the dark. His courtiers called him
a Solomon ; but even in the prime of his years he
was a Solomon in his dotage. His government,
during the former period of his reign, was not so
much an ineffective government as no government
at all. Even in matters ecclesiastical, on which
alone he felt strongly, and where the Protestant
nobility had apprehended a tightening of the rein,
his tyranny was exercised vicariously ; and there
were Jesuits enough in his dominions to prevent
any opportunity from passing unused. The Emperor himself only established systems of repres-
sion in order to permit them to be violated on the
morrow ; ten, twenty ordinances were at times sent
forth from the chancery in a single case, and commission after commission was issued to inquire
into the causes of their non-observance, till in the
end the matter was allowed to drop. In Bohemia
itself, where he caused the Utraquist Consistory to
be filled with Catholic clergy, the ordinances of
that consistory were persistently ignored ; and,

except in Vienna and some of the larger Austrian towns, the relations between the faiths remained in reality unchanged. Yet it was to these matters that Rhodolph directed the remnant of energy left to a naturally intelligent mind. The duties of his imperial position he utterly neglected; and during the great struggle in the Netherlands the troops neither of the King of Spain, nor of the King of Spain's rebels, respected the frontier; though the King was the Emperor's kinsman and ally, while the United Provinces legally formed an integral part of the Empire. Of his Hungarian kingdom half had thrown off nominal as well as actual allegiance; while his Bohemian subjects bearded his ordinances at his palace gates. The finances of his administration speedily fell into inseparable disorder; yet his personal extravagances, his taste for horses which he never rode, for pictures over which he mused in sullen solitude, for every curiosity or abnormity of science, art, and mechanical ingenuity, knew no bounds. (His collections are said to have been valued at seventeen millions of florins.) Then, as his mind gave way, he left the control of everything to the vilest of favourites; among others, to his body-servant, one Philip Lang, a vile minion, characterised by all the sensuality and recklessness of

a Cæsarean freedman : who sold offices in court,
army, and state ; who took bribes from foreign
princes ; who interfered in the administration of
justice, mismanaged the imperial domains, amassed
a large fortune by every kind of extortion, and
ultimately, though brought to trial, seems to have
escaped his appropriate earthly meed. (¹²)   Meanwhile the Emperor sat in his chamber, where perpetual silence was enjoined, dreaming over the
horoscopes of foreign ambassadors (the single kind
of inquiry which he was interested in addressing
to them), gazing at his treasures and toys, and
only varying his state of imbecile vacancy by fits
of furious passion, when he would hurl drinking-
cups at those who ventured to break his golden
rule.   Thus he is described to us in the year 1609
by another Italian visitor, the Tuscan Daniel
Eremita, whose interesting sketch of his German
travels offers a striking picture of many of its
courts and princes on the eve of the Thirty Years'
War. (¹³)   (The journal to which I refer is printed,
and I remember seeing a copy in the University
Library at Glasgow.)

For the first, and for the last, time in the history
of the House of Austria, that house recognised the
necessity of uniting against its chief, unless he
would consent to waive part, at least, of the rights

for the exercise of which he had been proved hopelessly unfit. About the commencement of the seventeenth century, the Emperor's melancholy, deepened by the influence of his astrological speculations, had assumed the natural phase of a belief in his approaching assassination. A Capuchin was sent to pray for his deliverance from the devils tormenting him ; but so capricious was the Emperor's mania that, as he declared, the monk's prayers added to his afflictions. Then he was approached by his brother next in age, the Archduke Matthias, who convinced himself, but not the Emperor, of the necessity of providing the latter with a coadjutor. Not even a successor could Rhodolph be brought to designate, although Pope Clement VIII. promised his acquiescence in the Emperor's choice, while Spain (now under the pacific sceptre of Philip III.) merely manifested a preference for Matthias' younger brother, the Archduke Albert, afterwards sovereign of the loyal Netherlands. But the pressure put upon the unmanageable recluse seems to have exercised the very contrary effect to that designed. He was stirred from his lethargy to a fitful endeavour at asserting his sovereign power in his realms of Bohemia and Hungary ; and this endeavour naturally took the direction of an attempt to extirpate the heresy

which had spread over the length and breadth
of both. The result was, that Hungary threw
herself into the ever-open arms of the Turk ;
and that the new allies advanced upon the
Austrian dominions.   Desolation threatened
Vienna ; while at Prague the Emperor had sunk
back into his usual apathy among his crucibles
and telescopes.([14])

The critical moment had arrived, when the
cadets of the house must take its future into
their own hands. They agreed to urge upon the
Emperor the appointment of Matthias as his
coadjutor.   Cunning, as we know, is the refuge
of the imbecile and of the monomaniac ; and
Rhodolph answered the demand first by evasions,
and then by alternately expressing his desire to
retire into a monastery, like Charles V. ; or to
marry in his old age, like Philip II.   The
archdukes hereupon, in the famous compact of
1606, which decided the destinies of the House
of Austria, agreed to acknowledge Matthias as
the head of the family ; and Spain and her
former candidate, Archduke Albert, sent in their
consent.   The conjuncture had arisen which
might have been foreseen from the commencement of Rhodolph's fatal reign.   To secure the
adherence of the Austrian estates against their

legitimate sovereign, Matthias was obliged to grant them the fullest concessions in religious matters. And, conversely, the Bohemians, whose crown had been left to Rhodolph, forced from him the famous *Letter of Majesty*, that great charter of their religious liberties, in defence of which they afterwards committed the act which opened the Thirty Years' War.

Matthias, as Häusser says, had called spirits which he could not lay.([15])   He tore even Bohemia from his unhappy brother's clutch; but before, in 1619, his seven years' reign came to a close amidst the flames of the Bohemian outbreak, he had been forced in his turn to resign his actual power into the hands of a coadjutor.   This coadjutor was Archduke Ferdinand, of the Styrian line, the pupil of the Jesuits, the early friend and close kinsman of Maximilian of Bavaria (now the head of the Catholic League), the trusted ally of Spain, and the hope of Rome and of all Catholic Europe.   Uniting in his hands all the dominions of the German Habsburgs, and assured of the imperial throne, Ferdinand prepared to struggle for the only one of the crowns of Matthias which seemed likely to elude his grasp, the crown of Bohemia.

And now, to recur to my former expression,

the cycle is complete; and Ferdinand II. enters,
under widely different conditions indeed, but
with virtually the same ends, upon a resumption
of the task of Charles V. No longer monarch
of Spain, but in close and confidential alliance
with Spain, the head of the House of Austria
undertakes to crush out heresy, and to establish
a monarchy which, from Baltic to Adriatic,
shall be one in allegiance and one in faith.
Ferdinand I. had been forced to relinquish the
thought of continuing the uncompromising policy
of his great brother; Maximilian II., soft of
heart and feeble of action, had abandoned it;
Rhodolph II. and Matthias had against their will
let the vessel drift further and further in the
same direction. Ferdinand II., a man devoid of
genius but strong of will, consciously resumed
what seemed to have become a hopeless task.
When, during the reign of Matthias, he had
been elected successor to the Bohemian crown,
he had sworn on the Scriptures to respect the
privileges of his future estates. But there are
oaths and oaths; and the same Ferdinand had
sworn before the altar of the Blessed Virgin at
Loretto—sworn before her as his generalissima,
as if he had been himself a soldier of the army
of Saint Ignatius—that he would, at the risk

of his life, purify his hereditary duchies from
heresy. For once we have so striking an anecdote on unexceptionable authority—on that of
his confessor, the Jesuit Father Lämmermann.([16])
Nowhere, as far as history knows, had he registered the vow that, by conquering heresy, as
Charles V. had conquered it in the Smalcaldic
War, he would recover the power which his great
ancestor had held during the interval between
victory and rout. But there are undertakings
which need to be consecrated by no affirma-
tion; and by his actions, consistent and progressive, Ferdinand's resolve sufficiently declared
itself.

The proofs of this assertion, which I hold that
history is able to punish, I hope in part to indi-
cate in my second lecture. To-night, if I have
not already exhausted your patience, I propose
to conclude with a brief view of the character,
and antecedents of the Prince, in whose person the
House of Austria made the great attempt which
constitutes the essence of the first part of the
Thirty Years' War; and which provoked that
opposition, whose allies in their turn revolutionised
the character of the struggle. For if it is possible
to recognise what Ferdinand II. was, and what
he intended to be, and how his action was con-

sciously conceived in the spirit of a steadfast
determination,—part, at all events, of the history
of the great war itself, may assume that aspect
of unity under which alone the main course of
the most complicated of European conflicts can
become intelligible.

Ferdinand was the eldest son of Archduke
Charles, Duke of Styria, and of his consort Mary,
a sister of Duke William of Bavaria.   In the
first two volumes of Hurter's expansive work on
Ferdinand II. and his parents, will be found an
almost embarrassing multitude of details from
which to form an opinion of the latter.   Charles
seems to have been a favourite of his kindly
father, the Emperor Maximilian, whose tender-
ness towards his younger sons led him to the
impulsive, but, from a political point of view, very
questionable step of breaking up the Austrian
dominions in their behalf.

(It is the good fortune of the House of Austria
that the very errors of its chiefs are apt to
provoke a species of sympathy, without necessi-
tating, as in the apologists of similar proceedings
on the part of the acknowledged founders of
Prussian greatness, an angry tone of defiance as
well as defence.)

Unlike his Imperial sire, Charles was above

suspicion in his loyalty towards Rome; and it was he who invited the Jesuits into his backsliding Styrian duchy.([17]) · He settled them there, in a college of their own, in his capital of Grätz, bidding them be of good cheer, though they came as sheep among wolves, and trust to his fatherly protection. According to a common tradition, the sheep in question were designated by the multitude as a black brood from Bavaria. In other words, their introduction was naturally, though it would seem erroneously, ascribed to the influence of Charles's consort Mary, scion of the orthodox branch of the House of Wittelsbach. This lady was one of those women who seem sent to demonstrate, by way of supererogation, the self-evident proposition, that a high intellectual efficiency is not incompatible with the charm attaching to the appropriate performance of the universally admitted duties of womanhood. (In religion, as in politics, women, if they choose a side, have been known to adhere to it with a consistency which throws into the shade the consistency of men; and a counterpart of Maria, in her devoted attachment to the teachings of the Jesuits, has been found in Magdalena Sibylla, the consort of John George of Saxony, and the most determined among the female champions of uncompromising Lutheran orthodoxy. If Maria brought up her son in fidelity to an Order which at last transferred its patronage to a more promising *protégée*, Magdalena Sibylla spared neither prayers nor curses against the Emperor and the Catholics—individually and collectively; and when John George at last resolved to accept the alliance of Gustavus Adolphus, encouraged her lord by an enthusiasm which it is more than doubtful whether he ever brought himself to share.) However, Charles was unable to second the operations of his monastic friends with all the warmth which his consort and himself felt towards them. The necessity of defending his frontiers against the Turk obliged him to hold a gentle rein over his refractory estates. But the activity of the fathers was irrepressible, and derived a powerful support from the foundation of the University of Grätz, which the piety of the Archduke delivered into their hands. It was not, however, here, but in the neighbouring Bavarian University of Ingolstadt, that Ferdinand spent those years when the seed of opinions is usually sown in the mind of man. Ingolstadt was, like Grätz, a Jesuit University; but its theological eminence dated from times preceding the foundation of the great Order. Was it not Ingolstadt which had sent

forth the most redoubtable disputant of the day
in Dr. Eck, to confute the Austin friar of the
mushroom University of Wittenberg? But under
the influence of the Jesuits and their educational
zeal, Ingolstadt had entered upon a new phase
of prosperity, and numbered among both its
teachers and its students Catholics from all
countries of Europe, from England among the
rest. ([18])   Over its halls hung the protecting ægis
of the Duke of Bavaria; and among its alumni
was his son Maximilian, afterwards the first
Elector of Bavaria, known in patriotic history
by the well-earned title of "the Catholic." For
Maximilian was to stand forth as the consistent
champion of Rome during the entire course of
the Thirty Years' War; nor can any character
in the history of that struggle be said to surpass
his in firmness or in sagacity. As a politician
he judiciously advanced the interests of his house
by taking advantage of the necessities as well
as of the successes of the House of Austria.
The *Basilicon Doron* which he bestowed upon his
son Ferdinand Maria was better warranted by
performance than the gift of his contemporary,
James VI. of Scotland, to his heir. "*Prudentia
propria imperantis virtus est*" (The proper virtue
of princes is prudence): this was one of the

lessons which Maximilian both enforced upon
his son and practised himself throughout a reign
of well-nigh three-score years.([10])   As a student he
appears to have surpassed his cousin Ferdinand,
both in the demonstrative fervour of his religiosity,
and in the display of general ability ; but Ferdinand, too, was regarded as a youth of more
than ordinary princely promise.   After his father's
decease, and during the ensuing regency of his
mother, he continued to pursue his studies at
Ingolstadt, faithful, at all events in academic
contests, to the device which he had chosen on
his departure from Grätz, (and which reappears
on all his coins,) "*Legitime certantibus.*"   It was
not till 1596, that he actually assumed the administration of his inheritance, which had by
that time been augmented (through the exertions
of his mother) by the accession of part of the
Tyrol ; while the same sagacious princess had
further advanced the importance of her dead
husband's line, by marrying her daughter Anna
to King Sigismund of Poland.

As far as we can judge from a review of
Ferdinand's bearing during his whole career, he
was one of those whom education early moulds to
a fixed type ; whose manhood begins at school
and lasts till the grave.   The strong but not

narrow system of his Jesuit teachers, and the
desire of his mother (evidenced by her correspondence) to keep him as free as possible from the
distracting influence of frivolous pursuits, combined
to render him serious and self-possessed from an
early age, but not with the gloominess of Philip of
Spain or of his uncle Rhodolph II. The details
of his private life are pleasing ; he was in particular attached to the most humanising of the
arts, music ; and, in this respect at all events,
was a true Austrian. Against his personal morality the busy inventiveness of a scandalous
age found no charges to advance. Sober, tem-
perate, and chaste ; strict in the observance of his
religious duties, as well as active in the performance
of the tasks of political life, he was well fitted for
a career of action and endurance. Such men as
Ferdinand and Maximilian, and on the Protestant
side the lion's brood of the House of Weimar,—
brought up under different circumstances, but on
similar principles, by an equally admirable mother,
—stand forth luminously, in spite of their moral
or intellectual defects, from among the drinking
and dicing confraternity of the German princes
of their day.([20]) And it is to their education, conducted under a mother's eye, whether by Jesuit
fathers or Lutheran divines, that we may ascribe

something of their stedfastness, of their energy, and of their confidence in a cause.

Yet fanaticism only too often prevails in its struggles with natural humanity and with an education sound within its limits—and Ferdinand II. was a fanatic. From his first proceedings on his assumption of the government over his paternal heritage, to the day when he sanctioned the assassination of Wallenstein, he never scrupled to postpone every other consideration to those which seemed to him identical,—the interests of the Catholic faith and the interests of his house. Ferdinand was not, like Philip II., a tyrant; but in the uncompromising rigour of his measures he only fell short of the Spaniard, because it is rarely that those opportunities occur of writing a name in letters of blood, which were mysteriously offered to Alva's master.

Ferdinand began his government in Styria, Carinthia, and Carniola, with the fixed resolve to extirpate heresy from these his hereditary dominions. And he succeeded. He refused pointblank to renew the privileges of the nobility; and then, after, as it were, consecrating himself to his mission by his famous journey to Rome and Loretto, set straightway about the execution of his task. A term was set to all Protestant preachers

D

for quitting his dominions ; another to the patrons of livings for nominating Catholic priests to the vacancies; and a third ordinance prohibited all sectarian books and the granting of civil rights to heretics. Then, a commission was appointed for the full restoration of the ancient faith ; exile or death (for no quibble and no *tu quoque* will avail to free these proceedings from a charge which their author would have scorned to evade) awaited the recalcitrants.([21]) Ferdinand's hereditary dominions were purified,—purified, as was Bohemia when after the expulsion of the Winter King he secured her crown ; and the House of Austria, after the impotence of a Ferdinand, the aversion of a Maximilian, and the oscillations of a Rhodolph and a Matthias, had at last a prominent membe: in whom Spain and the Holy See would recognise an uncompromising ally.

The first step had been taken, and taken with incontestable success. The next was the overthrow of the system of concession upon which Matthias, acting under the advice of his minister Cardinal Klesel, believed himself freed to govern in Austria proper. Klesel was, with the consent of Spain and the Pope, overthrown by a *coup d'état* in the Russian style of palace-revolutions.([22]) After his minister had been wafted away into the

safe mountains of Ferdinand's faithful Tyrol, Matthias, ever ready to give way to pressure, became
a passive instrument in the hands of his brothers.
Supported by the unanimous assent of the Archdukes to his succession to all the crowns of
Matthias, Ferdinand, during the closing years of
the former Emperor's reign, demeaned himself as
virtual ruler of all the hereditary dominions of the
House.   Among these hereditary dominions (if I
may thus lightly pass over one of the most difficult
of historical questions) Bohemia was only *practically* to be reckoned ;([28]) but, in spite of a protest,
and by means of a delusive oath, Ferdinand secured
his election as successor of Matthias at Prague ;
and in Hungary, where the case was similar, he
achieved the same result a little later, in 1617.
Thus in this memorable year the hopes of the
Catholic party had been apparently consummated
by the re-union of all the German and other
dominions of the Austrian branch of Habsburg in
the person of the Styrian Archduke.   Could he, to
crown all, secure his election to the Imperial throne,
the work of a century might at last be undone.
The work of a century ;—for it was in this year
1617 that the Elector of Saxony (under the
influence of his court-preacher, and doubtless
with the secondary intention of an anti-Calvinistic

demonstration) ordered the celebration of the First Centenary of the Reformation !(24) Another year, and the war had broken out; yet another, and Ferdinand, while grasping the Imperial, seemed to have lost the Bohemian crown.

I would that time permitted me to dwell, however briefly, upon the general aspect of that theatre on which the policy of the House of Habsburg, directed once more by a hand as tenacious, though not as supple, as that of Charles V., was during thirty eventful years to struggle for mastery over a changing combination of elements, before which it was at last to succumb in hopeless collapse. In lieu of a survey, I am forced to content myself with a single *caveat*. Such a war as this is not to be laid to the charge of individual or of dynasty. As we stand aghast in contemplating the real significance of that word *war*, we are willing to confess that even the great struggle known as the Revolt of the Netherlands is not in this sense to be charged upon Philip of Spain. For most assuredly every historical event, and every series of events, has part of its being in the past, in the development of which the freewill of human agents only shares as a co-operative, though a potent, factor. And so in the history of the Thirty Years' War, to whose torrent the

Netherlands' Revolt itself only added a tributary stream. Had it not been for the dynastic ambition of the House of Austria, says one historian, the German princes would have felt secure in the possession of their prized " liberty," and the Bohemian estates·would not have been driven by the violation of their Great Charter into their fatal outbreak. Had it not been for the thoughtless daring of the Elector Palatine, suggests another, the Bohemians, being without the hope of securing the support of the Protestant Union of which he was the head, would have come to terms with the prince in whose election to their crown they had formerly acquiesced. Had it not been for the timorous half-silence of King James I. of England, says a third, his son-in-law would not have dared to seize the fatal prize. And again, was it not the determination of Maximilian the Catholic to benefit by the false step of the adversary, whose electoral dignity and dominion he desired, which brought the League into the field and saved Austria on Bavaria's account ? Every one of these views is correct ; but correct only in so far as it assigns its due share to each element in the outbreak and first progress of the European struggle. The operation of other elements supervenes ; and, antecedently to all, there remains the fact, that the basis

of the peace which had been maintained in the
empire for nearly a century, was a religious compromise which neither side looked upon as permanent; that this compromise had been hateful to
Pope and Catholics ever since Charles V. had in
impotent resignation washed his hands of its conclusion ; and that its provisions had been practically
violated by the gradual advance of Protestantism
over the unnatural boundaries assigned to it ; while
a Catholic reaction had essayed to countermine
what it was unable to confront. Ferdinand II.
was the first openly and distinctly to announce the
resumption of the struggle which must end, whatever its result, in the contemptuous overthrow of
the compromise in question. For he, who has been
called "the pupil of the Jesuits," was such in no
vulgar sense. The Jesuits were the adequate
representatives of the great Catholic reaction ;
and of that reaction their pupil was at once the
child and the champion.

And this is what seems to me the meaning of a
phrase not less true than strange—"the lost opportunity of the Reformation." It was the lost
opportunity of consummating a national unity on
the basis of a religious agreement while such an
agreement was possible, and on the basis of the
remedy of abuses, while the best friends of the

Church were ready to acknowledge and deplore them as such. It was not all the Popes of the former half of the sixteenth century who would have been willing or able to withstand an *Eirenicon*, insisted upon by such an Emperor as Charles V. Nor was it Luther (as might be proved from his conduct at a critical moment) who would have at all times disdained it.[25] Charles V. deliberately—not otherwise—chose a different path; he failed in his endeavour to reach the desired goal ; and on a rotten foundation was erected a temporary superstructure without principle and without prospect of performance. The House of Austria, in its days of weakness, granted just enough to lose its last chance of preserving what it attempted to retain. Ferdinand II. renewed the great attempt of his ancestor to recover, and more than recover, *all.* His failure in the end was absolute ; but he, too, was encouraged by temporary success. For the Thirty Years' War was at one point of its course to raise the House of Austria to a pinnacle of power to which it had been a stranger since the epoch of Charles V.'s *Interim ;* but the transitory triumph was to be followed by an abasement lower than that of his Innsbruck flight. The Empire, which Ferdinand had hoped to unite in faith and allegiance, was to become a camping-ground for the hosts of nearly every European nation—of his self-seeking allies as well as of his rapacious enemies. It was to be shorn of fair lands for the benefit of Frenchman and of Swede ; and the solution of the ecclesiastical question was to be reached in a compact which sealed the discomfiture of his political ambition and religious zeal. But Ferdinand II. had died before the day when the territorial autonomy of the princes of the Empire was acknowledged as a principle of international law, and when the head of the House of Austria entered into a solemn treaty which the Holy See scorned to acknowledge.

LECTURE II.

SINCE monarchy has been a form of human government, there have probably occurred few reigns of which the opening was not, in this quarter or in that, believed to constitute the one heaven-sent opportunity of sovereign and people. To the reader even of the history of the Roman Cæsars there is, I think, something touching in the confidence with which an empire hails the young Apollo, destined, according to its belief, to convert into golden fulfilment the relics of hope left after the disappointments of the past. So, too, we are fain to sympathise with the French nation, deeming itself young again, as a Francis I. radiant with many of the more specious graces, and with all the more pleasant vices of his people, seems about to lead it on to its new era; or with our own ancestors, as they joyously behold their Henry VIII., armed with all the accomplishments of his age, and eager to tilt in tournament before the eyes of Europe, leap upon the throne laboriously built up and buttressed by the labours of a sour and unloved sire. It was under no such acclamations that Ferdinand II. entered upon his apparently hopeless task. His hereditary dominions indeed had been constrained by his relentless rigour into submission ; Styria and her sister-duchies had been ranged with the faithful Tyrol on the side of his desperate cause. But both Lower and Upper Austria were only watching their opportunity to enforce demands which his difficulties must oblige him to concede. Bohemia (and with her Moravia, Silesia, and the Lusatias) stood barred against his entry, and exulted in her chain of supposed alliances,—extending from the malcontent Austrian estates through her King designate to the Union of the Protestant Princes, the States of the United Provinces, and the sovereign of the British isles. Of France the policy had been pacific ever since the death of Henry IV. ; it was no longer directed by a prince who had declared that he would in no case permit the growth of the House of Austria ; and whose advance had, according to his own account, been solely delayed by his doubts whether his German allies could do aught but sleep and drink.(26) Yet it was from its alliance with France that the Protestant Union

had, in the days of the treaty of Hall, derived
its encouragement to preliminary action; and in
the end the traditionary foreign policy of that
monarchy must prevail over a reaction not even
supported by the authority of a regnant prince.
In the Scandinavian north, Gustavus Adolphus
was lending a gracious ear to the suit of the
Bohemian estates for the assistance of Sweden
and for her intervention to secure the goodwill
of the Hanseatic towns; and if Christian IV. of
Denmark was at this particular epoch coquetting
with Ferdinand's only foreign allies, Spain and
Poland, it was merely in the spirit of rivalry
against Sweden that he was permitting himself
these demonstrations—a rivalry which might at
any time show itself, as it actually showed itself,
in an endeavour to anticipate Gustavus Adolphus
in the championship of the Protestant cause.
Even in Italy, the quarrel between Venice and the
Pope, and the hostility between Savoy and Spain,
placed another naval and another military power
among the ranks of Ferdinand's opponents. And
in the east, the Turkish terror was looming nearer
than ever; while from Transylvania the redoubtable Bethlen Gabor was hurrying to the walls of
Vienna, there to hold rendezvous with Thurn,
who, as the leader of the Bohemian rebels, was

already approaching the Austrian capital from the north.([27])

Such were some of the elements of the political conjuncture, when Ferdinand, the lord of seven revolted provinces, the virtually " abdicated" (the verb is thus significantly construed by the prag- matists of the time) King of Bohemia, and candi- date for the Imperial throne, for which it seemed as if his own subjects would hinder him from proffering his suit, was bearded in his castle at Vienna by a handful of citizens. They demanded the immediate grant of their religious privileges, and enforced their suit by plucking with offensive familiarity at the jerkin on their " Nandel's" breast. He was saved from the importunate solicitations of his dear Viennese by the sudden arrival of a troop of horse ; and with this episode, famous in pictorial history, the crisis of his situation seemed to have passed. Before the year (1619) was out, he had reached Frankfort ; and on the 9th of September (N.S.) he held in his hand the sword of Charlemagne, while the three Spiritual Electors placed on his head the Imperial crown.([28])

Occupat extremum scabies. The Protestant Union, instead of venturing upon open resistance, had taken refuge in a foolish intrigue. Its chief, the Elector Palatine, was endeavouring to turn aside

Maximilian of Bavaria, the head of the Catholic
League, from the Austrian alliance, by dangling
before his sober eyes the prospect of the Imperial
crown.   Even had the prospect been other than
delusive, Maximilian, as of old Frederick the Wise
(or, as according to rumour, a descendant of
Frederick's under similar circumstances in our
own day), might have been relied upon to decline
the offer by an appeal to his own reputation
for common sense.[29]) But Ferdinand (and here
again we are irresistibly reminded of Charles V.'s
interview with Henry VIII., which so fatally took
the meaning out of the blatant festivities of the
Field of the Cloth of Gold) had on his way to
Frankfort found time to visit his cousin Maximilian, and to bind him by a promise that, if the
Union should openly support the Bohemians, the
League would openly support the House of
Austria.   In any case Maximilian was not an
Elector, but only anxious to become one.   How
then are we to explain, under the circumstances
of Ferdinand's candidature, the ultimate unanimity
of votes in his favour?

It can hardly require to be pointed out how
fallacious would be the view which should assume
the Empire to have been at this time divided
into Protestants and Catholics in the same pro-

portion as at the date of the Smalcaldic War; or, that this division corresponded to that into opponents or supporters of the House of Austria. For, confining ourselves to the princes (though, were we to take into account the other classes of estates, the preponderance would, of course, be still stronger on the same side), the Protestants were at the commencement of the Thirty Years' War considerably superior to the Catholics, both in number and in power. But, even among the former, there was in general little disposition to disturb a state of things which had hitherto left them in possession of their cherished "liberty," in other words, of their territorial supremacy in matters spiritual as well as temporal. For this was the great maxim of the Reformation of the sixteenth century, which, as in England, had been in Germany a struggle, not for religious liberty, but for religious truth ; that he who had the power was not only himself to believe after the fashion which commended itself to him, but to benefit others by imposing his belief upon them. Translated into the pragmatic jargon of the times, this maxim was expressed as the famous "*Cujus regio ejus est religio*"—whose the soil is, his are the souls thereon. What more logical, and yet what more inviting to a *reductio ad absurdum*, than this? The weak government of Charles V.'s successors had intensified that sense of territorial absolutism, which, in uncongenial conjunction with the brutal manners of the times, made most of the princes regard themselves as popes, and demean themselves as sultans, in their dominions. In the sixteenth, and even in the seventeenth century, the custom of subdividing the paternal inheritance among the sons, continued very generally to obtain among the princes and high nobility of the Empire. The result of this system of subdivision, while it infinitely complicates the history of the situation, and leaves a summary survey of it out of the question, at the same time accounts for the variety of relations in matters political and religious, which we find prevailing in the several lines of the same houses. The House of Wittelsbach had long separated into two main branches, whose representatives now confronted one another as the heads of Union and League. The head of the elder branch was scheming for a royal crown, while the head of the younger was intent upon securing for himself his kinsman's electoral hat. The jealousy and ambition of this younger (or Bavarian) line was not the less active, because its commencement dated from the middle of the previous

century. In Saxony the well-known division into
the Ernestine and Albertine lines had been further
subdivided. Both of these lines were Lutheran;
but while the Ernestine (which had little to lose
and everything to gain) developed into a determined brood of devout conspirators, the Albertine
(to which Charles V. had transferred the electorate)
was traditionally anxious to secure its tenure by
an attitude of loyalty towards the House of
Habsburg. Such had been its policy, after the
death of Maurice, under the reign of the prudent
Elector Augustus; from him the government had
passed into the hands of Christian II., whom
Daniel Eremita, when the course of his travels
led him to Torgau, found generally drunk and
always incapable; but this potentate (one of the
few among their sovereigns for whom the inven-
tive loyalty of Saxon historians has failed to
suggest an appropriate epithet) had quaffed his
last cup before the outbreak of the war. John
George I. (who, like Maximilian of Bavaria, survived the entire course of the war) ruled in his
stead a prince cautious even to timidity, but
to whom I think Mr. Bryce in his admirable essay
has done great injustice, in designating him as
"the most infamous of his infamous house."
At the commencement of the war, John George

was, no doubt, entirely under the influence of his
court-preacher, the notorious Hoë von Hoënegg;
a Viennese by birth, and devoted to the service
of the House of Austria and to the extermination
of Calvinism.   Thus the Union, led by Frederick
of the Palatinate, could place no hopes in John
George and his mentor, in whose estimation a
Calvinist kicked the beam against a Papist, and
whose services to his own faith are not inaptly
summed up in one of the songs of the war;

> " Though my religion's true as gold,
>   I've done it damage manifold ; "

and the policy of the most powerful of the
Electors during the first part of the war may be
summed up as an endeavour to support Austria,
without sacrificing his character as a Protestant
prince, and without expending money or men,
except under a more than adequate guarantee.([30])
Similarly, in Brandenburg, the Elector Joachim II.
(a prince in the style of the eighteenth century,
whose system of government redounded to, the
exclusive profit of the Jews) had been succeeded
by Hans Sigismund, who had become a Calvinist
and joined the Union ; but upon him followed, in
1619, George William, whose consort converted him
(and implicitly his electorate) to Lutheranism,

E

while his minister, Schwarzenberg, made him a creature of the Imperial policy. The fruits of these endeavours were to become apparent when George William's brother-in-law, Gustavus Adolphus, after his invasion of the empire, was forced to stand parleying with his "natural ally" as to the admission of his troops to a Brandenburg fortress, and was thus prevented from saving the bulwark of Protestant Christendom, Magdeburg, out of the clutches of Tilly. Hesse, whose name so memorably connects itself with the early struggles of the Reformation, in the days of her high-souled landgrave Philip, had by him been parted into the two lines of Cassel and Darmstadt. The former of these, Calvinist and true, from first to last, to the traditional active and advanced policy of the House, had joined the Union ; while the latter, though also Protestant, leant towards the Emperor, always favoured his policy, and was throughout the war a false friend or an open adversary of the Protestant opposition. A similar contrast is observable among the princes of Baden, and in the house of Guelph in Brunswick and Lüneburg.

These instances may suffice to illustrate the divided and uncertain state of the Empire, when the rash ambition of Frederick of the Palatinate

threw down in its midst the brand of war. The
iconoclastic fanaticism of his court-preacher, and
his own inability to control the rude and turbulent
spirit of his new subjects, would have of themselves made it impossible for him to consolidate
his usurpation; moreover, he was deserted by all,
or nearly all the allies upon whose support he
had, against the better judgment of others, permitted himself to calculate. Sweden alone was
of use, by keeping Poland employed; but the
Dutch excused themselves by offensively excellent
arguments; King James shook his head, and en-
joyed in the affairs of his son-in-law a satisfaction,
rarely permitted to him in his own, of being wise
after the event: the Transylvanian was bought
off by a few tons of gold;—and France recom-
mended a conference. The Union went so far as
to assemble in order to debate the situation of
its chief; and proposed to itself three main, and
thirty-two subsidiary questions. In short, as a
modern historian of the Bohemian War has
observed, we find among the allies of the unhappy
Frederick nothing but impotence, obscurity, irre-
solution, fear, and selfishness.([31])

Frederick's weakness was Ferdinand's opportunity. Purchasing the support of Saxony by
giving up to her Elector one of his provinces,

and that of the League by pledging another to its chief the Bavarian duke, and confiding in the promise of troops from Spain, the Emperor crushed the Winter-king. Frederick and his fair wife, whose growth Ralegh had tenderly watched from his prison, whose beauty Wootton had sung in his sweetest strains, and who, in her days of misfortune was again to become the darling of the English nation, were homeless fugitives. The Union ended its career by a treaty of virtual neutrality, and obtained its epitaph in a stave of the day, to the effect that,

> " While peace prevailed, they kept their force,
> Full closely joined both foot and horse,
> And did conclude a *Union ;*
> But war arrived—and lo ! 'twas gone ! "

By the help of the League, and its general, Tilly (an honest old savage, whom a recent refreshingly audacious attempt has failed to whitewash into a Christian hero), Ferdinand was master of Bohemia. (³²)

There could be no doubt as to the fate in store for the vanquished kingdom ; and to this day she bears the traces of her reconciliation to the dominion and the faith of the House of Austria. Yet I cannot agree with Müller's view, that the Bohemians are to be charged with the responsi-

bility of their country's sufferings. It has been
sagaciously observed by the present Emperor of
the French, that men are not justified in resorting
to unlawful means, when lawful will better suit
the purpose. The Bohemians had before them
the choice between submitting to Ferdinand, and
rescinding his election to their throne. They
chose the latter alternative; and herein they seem
to have made no fond calculation. True, they
played their venturous game badly; but they
could hardly have reckoned on so much weakness
in Frederick; so much tergiversation in James; so
much backwardness in the Dutch; and so much
cowardice in the Union. Nor could they have
anticipated so unparalleled, I feel almost inclined
to say so heroic, a determination in their opponent.
Ferdinand had alienated Upper Austria to Bavaria,
with small hope of speedily redeeming it (six
years, in fact, elapsed before he recovered this
province); and to Saxony he had permanently
sacrificed the Lusatias. Fortune had befriended
him when he was able to purchase the neutrality
of the Transylvanian, and to keep off the Turk.
Against such odds he had prevailed; and now
Bohemia was at his feet, Spanish troops were
pouring into the Palatinate, and the Union was
on the eve of a natural death.([33])

He used his victory without hesitation and
without mercy. The *Letter of Majesty* he cut
into shreds with his own hand; and then set
about the task of purifying Bohemia. It was a
purification to which history has no parallel.
Then he turned to Upper Austria, where there
ensued the terrible persecution of the years 1624
and 1625, and the suppression of the peasant's
revolt resulting from it. These transactions (upon
which time alone prevents me from dwelling) form
one of the most singular episodes in Ferdinand's
reign, or indeed in the history of the Austrian
dominions. ([34]) For you will remember that it
was this province of Upper Austria which Ferdinand had promised in pawn to his ally Maximilian.
Before he transferred it in performance of his
agreement, he was fain, with the aid of its future
occupant, to reduce it to a condition in which it
might be handed over without its encumbrances
of heresy.

The forces which the Emperor had been able
to hire on his own account—foreigners in the
main; for, said their commander, Bucquoi, "these
alone are to be trusted;"—had only contributed
in a small degree to the consummation of his
triumph. By the aid of the League, he had
conquered: but it was not to the League, nor to

its far-sighted chief, that he was minded to leave the development of the victory. The armed resistance of the Protestants had degenerated into a war of mercenaries led by outlaws; by such men as Christian of Anhalt, the real author of the Union, whose indefatigable activity could not be suppressed by the downfall of his schemes; and the terrible Mansfeld, "the Attila of the priests."([35]) But the fear of the results of Ferdinand's victory accomplished what the temptation of his difficulties had been unable to bring about; and, at the summons of the restless Christian IV of Denmark, the powers of Northern Europe (including England, Sweden, the United Provinces, and the German estates of the Lower-Saxon circle) had opened negotiations for an alliance. Of this alliance, the pretext was found in the rights of the fugitive ex-elector of the Palatinate, dispossessed by Ferdinand in favour of the Duke of Bavaria; but its motive we must seek in the terror inspired by the triumph of the House of Habsburg, and the way in which she was using that triumph. While, however, the Spaniards were pouring into the Palatinate, and while the Emperor was gathering his strength for another onward step in his consistent course, the counter-alliance halted, and then collapsed. Upon James I. of England rests, as we now know, the main responsibility of this fatal hesitation. In the teeth of his under-dertakings and promises, and in despite of the declared desires of his own subjects, James was amusing himself with the most notable of those operations of his favourite balancing power, which invariably ended in a slough of despond. Anxious to save the heritage of his daughter, he had devised, as the best means of securing this result, the project of sending his son to sue for the hand of a Spanish infanta. [36]

In the policy of Ferdinand there was no hesitation, and no balancing. While his adversaries were faltering over their engagements, he was arming for war on his own account. Given a disaffected dominion, and an empty treasury; the question was, how, except by miracle, an army could be created for their master. Wallenstein undertook to work the miracle. The Emperor's share in the scheme was the insertion of a condition, that the expenses of the army should be provided, not by the Imperial exchequer, but by the exactions from the Empire. In other words, Ferdinand bestowed his Imperial sanction upon the method of warfare hitherto pursued by Mansfield and the Protestant *condottieri*, and thus gave to the subsequent course of the struggle that impress, which is distinctive of the Thirty Years' War.

For, from this point, it is idle to regard that war as one between religions. If I read the character and proceedings of Wallenstein aright, it was he who breathed into the schemes of Ferdinand that vague and yet consistent grandeur, which marks their later developments as the creations of genius. Wallenstein was a dreamer; but he was neither the moonstruck madman, as which soon after his catastrophe, his figure was introduced upon the English stage; nor was he the benevolent visionary of some of the finest passages of Schiller's noble tragedy. His relation to Ferdinand was one which defies comparison; some points of resemblance might be found, if I may compare an ordinary man to a great, in the relation of Wolsey to Henry VIII. During the period up to Wallenstein's dismissal, the sovereign followed the inspiration of his *generalissimus;* and the servant was loyal to his master. Wallenstein doubtless desired and laboured to become a prince of the Empire, but always with a view to the interests of the Emperor; and it is herein that I trace some resemblance between the nature of his personal ambition, and that of Wolsey, when he aspired to the papal chair. Afterwards, the character of the relation changed; but it was in Ferdinand's mind that the fatal seed of doubt was first sown. Then, the pressure of friends and foes operated upon both; and the renewed connexion was severed by a deed of blood.

But it is of the operations in which Wallenstein acted as the loyal marshal of the House of Austria, that I am now speaking. Too little attention has, I think, until recently, been paid to the vast scheme by which Ferdinand and Wallenstein, in conjunction with Spain, intended to create a power for the House of Habsburg untasted even by Charles V., and for a parallel to which I know not where to seek, except in the proceedings of the great Napoleon. It is known now, when the leadership of the Protestant cause had been assumed by Christian IV. of Denmark, Wallenstein, at the head of the Imperial army, in conjunction with Tilly and the troops of the League, swept before him the forces of the Danish King, and of his German confederates. The whole Empire was now in their power; and the Danish deliverer was fain to take refuge in his islands, and to sue for any peace which would leave him a king. After this had been done, and after the two generals had completed their conquest by overrunning the Mecklenburgs and

Holstein, Wallenstein insisted upon occupying the former himself,—a proceeding not sufficiently accounted for by motives of personal ambition. For it was at the same time that Wallenstein was created by the Emperor, General of the Oceanic and Baltic seas. A doggrel rhyme of the day sneers at Wallenstein as an admiral sans ships; and a superficial view of this episode might seem to offer grounds for an adoption of the taunt. In truth, the assumption of this title marks the attempted realisation of the grandest, and by no means the most visionary of Wallenstein's schemes, in the interest of that prince of whom he had constituted himself the right hand.

It was a scheme to which, as I have indicated, the Spanish branch of the House of Habsburg was no stranger; and it implied the ruin of the trade of the United Provinces and of England, by a revival of the glories of the German Hansa under the Imperial protectorate. The Hanseatic towns were to abandon their attitude of neutrality in the war, their amicable relations with the Scandinavian kingdoms, and their freedom of trade. In return, they were to receive the monopoly of the Spanish commerce with the Indies. In other words, the principal trade of Europe was to be thrown into the hands of dependants of the

House of Habsburg; the *dominium maris Baltici et Oceani* was to be restored to the Hansa—but not to the Hansa in her ancient character of a league of German towns. It was this which gave to the siege of Stralsund (who clung to her alliance with Sweden), so transcendant a significance, of which the age was fully and deeply conscious. It was this which caused Wallenstein to swear that he would take the city, were she riveted with chains to the heavens (the expression is probable enough, even though it be. inefficiently authenticated). And it was for this reason that, when he failed, and when the other Hanseatic towns took courage from the success of their sister, to resist an advance which had been proved no longer irresistible, a cry of joy arose which seems still to echo in Lübeck's venerable halls and along Hamburg's crowded quays. "Never have eagles been known to swim; and he that essays to slide stones along the surface of the water, shall see them sink without fail. The sea recks not of the whips and the floggings of Xerxes; for it is not possible to hang, or behead, or drown the sea." There is in this Hanseatic *Jubilate* that smack of contemptuous pride and sturdy humour which is characteristic of a race of mariners; and it was of such a race that the men had sprung,

who, with the aid of Swedish and Scottish helpmates, stayed the triumphant advance of the
House of Austria, and hurled back the defiance
of her lieutenant. ([37])

Across the sea, Ferdinand's and Wallenstein's
conqueror was shortly to come. But before Gustavus Adolphus dashed from the Emperor's lips
the intoxicating cup, filled though it was with an
empire's grievances, the last drop had yet to be
added. The siege of Stralsund marks the limit
of Austria's advance ; the use to which that advance was to be put, becomes clear from the
Imperial edict promulgated in the same year, and
known to history as the *Edict of Restitution*.

This famous measure may be summarily described, as an attempt to restore the relations
between the Catholic and the Reformed Faiths
to the *status quo ante pacem*. In my former lecture,
I begged to recall to you the nature of that compact of Augsburg, of the year 1555, which served
as the basis of the hollow and uncertain peace
maintained in the Empire for nearly three-quarters
of a century. During that period, Protestantism
had advanced far beyond the limits which it had
reached at the date of the conclusion of the compact ; now, the Emperor Ferdinand was determined
to drive it back once more within its ancient

boundaries. All the sees, which since the peace of Augsburg had been sequestered by the Protestants, or filled with heretical administrators, were to be restored to the Catholic religion. That this was no sudden design on the part of the Emperor, is clear from the extremely significant circumstance, that, at the time when he secured the aid of John George by the cession of Lusatia, he had coupled with this the promise of leaving untouched the tenants of ecclesiastical domains in the Saxon circles. Saxony, having thus been bought off, with the aid of an exceptional concession of the very principle contended for, the Emperor could proceed at his ease elsewhere after the victories of Tilly and Wallenstein. Isolated instances of restitution occur as early as 1624; and in the conquered Palatinate, Bavaria had been permitted to proceed undisguisedly upon the principle of absolute spiritual lordship. But the edict which proclaimed the emperor's intention of restoring the *status quo* of 1555, and of establishing, as a principle of action, that *reservatum ecclesiasticum* which had been violated with impunity for three-quarters of a century, was not published till March 1629. Henceforth, however, no time was to be lost; and the commissioners entrusted with the execution of the edict

were directed, in case of resistance, to appeal for
aid · to the nearest army, whether Imperial or
Liguistic.

Those who hold that the justification of a
measure lies in its fidelity to the letter of the law,
may applaud the resolution which promulgated
this edict. Those who believe that treaties share
the fate of all things human, and accordingly
have a tendency to become obsolete before they
happen to be cancelled, will judge Ferdinand's
act to have been not the less despotic, because
he incontestably had legality on his side.

But this was not all. For it speedily became
apparent that the Emperor was not intent upon
the revival of an obsolete state of things, without a very practical determination in reference to
the present and the future. Already a recovered
bishopric and abbey had been given to one of his
sons, Leopold William, Bishop of Passau. It was
now determined to indulge this capacious pluralist
still further, by conferring upon him the two most
important archbishoprics of Northern Germany:
Bremen (on which Christian of Denmark had in
vain cast a loving eye) and Magdeburg (where
the loyal John George of Saxony's son had been
elected by the chapter, wise as it thought in its
generation, to fill the place of the outlawed

the second great crisis of his career, he, in
deference to the complaints of both Catholic and
Protestant estates, dismissed Wallenstein. We
may leave some of the more enthusiastic biographers of the latter to indite the usual tirades
against Austrian ingratitude; but the step was
a fatal one, and incontestably marks the close
of Ferdinand's progressive policy. There never
was a sounder argument than that of Wallenstein's
friends, when they reminded the Emperor that
the attack upon his general was in reality
directed against himself; and never a more significant word than that which the Duke uttered
as his sole comment upon his dismissal: "The
spiritus of the Elector of Bavaria prevails over
the *spiritus* of his Imperial Majesty." Ferdinand,
believing, as it seems to me, that there was no
serious danger of the Protestant Electors listening
to the invitations of the Swedish adventurer;
eager to defeat the intrigues of France with the
Catholic princes, and to secure once more his
endangered alliance with the latter; and intent,
above all, upon the election of his son as Roman
King,—gave way before the princes. *The lesser
dynastic end prevailed over the greater;* yet, for the
time, the Emperor was foiled even of what had
seemed to him an equivalent for such a sacrifice.

Wallenstein was dismissed; but the Emperor's son was not elected to the Imperial successorship. No error has ever more fatally avenged itself; for it was an abnegation by the Emperor of his surest, indeed his only means of carrying out his Imperial policy at a moment of unsurpassed importance in his career.[40] And the attempt to undo the error ended even more disastrously than the error itself.

Thus it comes to pass, that while the earlier part of the war is in a political sense complicated and hard to read, the second and third periods (frequently called the Swedish and Suedo-French wars) are from this point of view comparatively clear and intelligible. Gustavus Adolphus—of this there remains no doubt—aspired to no less a prize than the Imperial crown. But it was not his intention to wrest it from Ferdinand. Rather, it appears to result from his entire course of action, that he designed to carve out for himself with his sword a great territory, by the tenure of which he would become a great German prince, entitled at Ferdinand's death to claim the German crown, to which he should have been in the lifetime of the defeated Emperor appointed the successor. It is under this aspect, and under this alone, that his conduct of the war seems to me to become intelligible. The sack of Magdeburg—which, even were its captors freed from every stain of criminality, would remain a monstrous political blunder—threw Saxony into his arms; the victory of Breitenfeld placed the fate of the Empire in his power. Then, had he marched upon Vienna, it must have fallen. And so must the same city have fallen into the hands of the victors of Sadowa, and so must Rome into those of Hannibal after Cannæ. But, whatever we may think of the Prussians of our own day, neither Hannibal nor Gustavus were politicians of the event. Since it was not the primary object of the latter to gratify the readers of the *Swedish Intelligencer*, he preferred not to leave doubtful allies in his rear, while holding a triumphal entry into the cathedral of St. Stephen. He committed to the Saxons the care of Bohemia, where (as the discontented soldier of fortune in Schiller's *Camp of Wallenstein* so graphically describes it) "war seemed a joke, and there was little glory to get;" while at the head of his own troops he continued his march of conquest to Franconia and Bavaria. Everywhere he demeaned himself as the father of the countries which fell into his hands; at the Imperial city of Frankfort he held his court, surrounded by Protestant princes; and finally he

established himself in Maximilian's palace at
Munich, whence his sway virtually extended over
the whole of the Empire, with the exception of the
hereditary dominions of the House of Habsburg.([41])

And this was the foe whom Ferdinand, less
sagacious in his hour of triumph than when he
had seemed to lie at the mercy of his antagonists,
had believed himself entitled to despise; and
whose agent had been contemptuously excluded
as an interloper from the peace negotiations at
Lübeck, only two years before. The Swede had
sent before him an insolent demand "that the
Roman Emperor should take his army out of the
Roman Empire, and not in future maintain one
there." He had now taken care that his demand
had met with compliance. But Wallenstein yet
lived. Might not the genius of the House of
Habsburg yet revive it from the depths into which
it had been frustrated? Ferdinand induced him
to resume the command on the well-known terms
which amounted to an actual transfer of some of
the Imperial prerogatives to a subject. Wallenstein,
I think, understood Gustavus Adolphus. This
seems clearly proved by the strategy which the
former adopted, and which ultimately succeeded in
drawing the Swedish king out of his conquered
territories, to the battle-field of Lützen.

The *Te Deum* sung at Vienna and Madrid for the death of the arch-foe of the House of Habsburg was premature. For an enemy survived, who with deadly skill could carry on his work; and who could use the good as well as the evil fortune of the House for its ruin.

But the illustration of this and other features of the concluding part of the war I must unwillingly leave aside. The death of Gustavus threw the Protestant princes into the eager embrace of France; and Richelieu benefited by an event which ridded him of an ally too strong to be an instrument. It was Richelieu who ruined Wallenstein; who destroyed such mutual confidence as remained between him and the Emperor, and who drew round the dazzled general a network, of the impenetrability of which Wallenstein himself was hardly aware. Again, the Imperial victory of Nördlingen, which put an end to the Swedish protectorate over the South-west, became another of Richelieu's opportunities; for its result was the treaty of 1634 which made Bernard of Weimar, the Protestant general-in-chief, the lieutenant of France. It was then that the bitterness of disgust came over those princes who, like the Elector of Saxony, had been bound fast to the triumphant progress of Gustavus Adolphus; and that the

peace of Prague of 1635 restored their relations
to the Emperor, on the basis of a compromise, to
very nearly the footing on which they had stood
before the fatal Edict of Restitution. But the war
had long passed beyond the control of Emperor
and Electors.

Ferdinand II., accordingly, lived long enough to
end the quarrel which he had provoked in his hour
of triumph ; but not long enough to see the fire
extinguished of the European war into which that
quarrel had developed. When he died in 1637,
he left to his son Ferdinand III. a harvest, not yet
all gathered in, of Imperial and dynastic dangers
and difficulties ; while he had already sacrificed
the religious policy on behalf of which he had
incurred them.

Thus ends a reign of transcendent importance
in the history of the House of Austria. For the
struggle which Ferdinand III. was forced to continue for eleven years longer had become on his
part a purely defensive war, though it was necessarily carried on in part in the form of offensive
operations. Like his father, in faith a devout
Catholic, and like him unimpeachable in his personal morality, he had before him only one course
of political action, and was not, like Ferdinand II.,
called upon to choose between two paths. To save

what he *could* save out of the wreck and ruin of
the Imperial power, and to hold fast to every acre
to which he *could* hold of his dynastic inheritance,
was the plain yet hard task which Ferdinand III.
pursued with all the firmness of his character, and
all the doggedness of his race. And he was well
served by agents who are unforgotten in the
brilliant annals of Austrian diplomacy. Only, it is
no longer the dynastic schemes of the past which
the head of the House of Austria is able to pursue.
For the furtherance of those schemes the essential
elements have long vanished from the situation.
With the Swedes prolonging the war in the simple
intention of raising the price of their "satisfaction;"
with the French, under the direction of Richelieu's
successor Mazarin, plainly determined to establish
a permanent influence on the Rhine ; while even
Spain is anxious to hinder a peace in which the
United Provinces cannot fail to obtain a recognition
no longer to be denied them on any rational ground,
—Ferdinand III. has to watch and wait, anxious
to conclude peace, but cautious not to conclude it
before the right moment. At last, after five long
years, during which (as the relics at Osnabrück
and Münster help to tell us) the plenipotentiaries
seemed to have established themselves for an in-
definite series of negotiations, the peace is concluded.

Sweden and France are satisfied; the former with
money and land, and the coveted character of an
estate of the Empire; the latter, too, with German
territory, and with what she prizes still more
dearly, the opportunities of future interference.
Brandenburg on the one side, and Bavaria on the
other, each with her acquisitions, go rejoicing away.
The United Provinces, once a part of the Empire,
are recognised as independent; even Switzerland
has been allowed to sever the link which unites to
the Empire the ancient home of the Habsburgs.[42]

But it was not only sacrifices of land that had
been made, and virtual excrescences which had
been lopped off. Shorn and mutilated, the Empire
had moreover become a mere aggregate of independent territories, in which the sovereign authority
and the right of concluding alliances were left
to each individual prince. Their votes at the
Diet were henceforth to be decisive, instead of
deliberative; what was the Emperor now beyond
a president among his peers? And in religion,
except in the hereditary dominions of the House
of Austria, toleration was ensured to the three
rival creeds; while, as to the crucial question of
benefices, the settlement of Augsburg was con-
firmed in the *status* of its operation at a period
falling before the very first of the recoveries

made by Ferdinand II. on behalf of the Catholic
Church.

To conclude, then, by one more glance across
the eventful period, in which I have endeavoured
to trace some among the operations of the policy
of Charles V. and his successors. His attempt to
unite the greater part of Europe in a political
and religious consolidation, at the cost of imperil-
ling the integrity of Germany and disappointing
the hopes of the German nation, had been made
at a time when all the dominions of the House
of Habsburg were in the hands of a single prince.
After his retirement, the Spanish branch had
carried on the endeavour through Philip II. ; but
he, as all the world except himself came to acknowledge, had succumbed before the combined
resistance of his Netherlands and of England,
and before their alliance with regenerated France.
The House of Austria had, under Ferdinand II.,
in conjunction with Spain, once more resumed
the scheme. Step by step, with progressive consistency, and without shrinking from the most
tremendous risks, or from the most momentous
sacrifices, Ferdinand II. had advanced the cause
of Rome and of his dynasty. Wallenstein had
knocked at the portals of the North ; while the
Edict of Restitution had proclaimed the undoing

of a century's work as an accomplished fact to
the terrified princes. At this point, the triumphant
advance of the House of Austria was arrested;
and it was converted into defeat by the invasion
of Gustavus Adolphus, carried out with the co-
operation of France. Richelieu and Mazarin
drove home the wedge till it split the rotten tree;
and Ferdinand II. lived to renounce his policy
of aggression, and to point out to his successor
the means of saving what remained to be saved.

The House of Austria had for the last time
(to use a phrase which, however glibly it runs
on men's tongues, has nevertheless its historical
justification) endangered the balance of Europe.
Henceforth, her family of states is no longer
threatened by a resumption of the plans of
Charles V.; and the real danger to her peace
springs from other quarters, and in the first instance
from France alone. The Reformation has per-
formed its great political task of disintegrating
Europe; and the House of Habsburg has been
conquered in its attempt to revive its ideal of unity.
The balance of Europe becomes a convenient phrase
to be bandied about over green tables, around
which are assembled the representatives of states
no longer connected by any common interest.
Henceforth there is no alliance which is impossible;

no combination which is not on the cards. For the nations of Europe, though they learnt from the wars of the sixteenth and seventeenth centuries the futility of bloodshed in the name of religion, failed to perceive the worse than futility of dynastic ambition and dynastic wars. It was long before the truth began to dawn upon Europe—and who shall say that it has been accepted in its fulness in this our own day ?—that there is only one thing which can really maintain the balance of Europe, viz. the solidarity of the interests of her people. I believe that we have to thank the second French Empire for the word ; but the idea, Europe owes to the French Revolution and to the history of its results. For the French Revolution overcame the confederation of its opponents, not merely by the strength of its own enthusiasm, but because (as is becoming more clear from day to day) its continental opponents formed an ill-yoked alliance of self-seeking dynasties. The heir of the French Revolution was crushed, not by these dynasties, but by the uprising of the nations. What the Conference of Pilnitz had effected, was undone by the battle of Leipzig—the battle, in more senses than one, of the peoples.[48]

Germany herself had suffered, as no nation has suffered before or after, by a war of which it would be hazardous to charge the House of Austria with the original responsibility ; but which, had it not been for the policy of that House, could not have run such a course, or taken such an end. Sick and weary after the struggle, a devastated and depopulated land could hardly take account of its gains for thinking of what it had lost. But deep into the consciousness of the people, though not of all its dynasties,—for the House of Austria, for one, the era of religious tolerance had not yet even dawned,—had sunk the lesson : that the battle of moral and intellectual freedom is not to be fought on battle-fields, and that progress is not to be achieved by the aid of fire and sword. It was as if the spirit of the Reformation, before it became a religious controversy, had again pervaded the nation of its birth. In Germany's impoverished cities, in her ridiculed and ridiculous petty principalities, sprang up from the blood-drenched soil, very slowly and painfully, but very surely, the seed of her second and greater Renascence. Swedes and Frenchmen, Spaniards and Italians, hordes of foreign hirelings in the pay of the Emperor or of his foes, might have combined to decide her immediate political future ; might have meted out her territories, and curtailed her boundaries ; might even have served to fix the standard of her religious liberties. But to continue the work of the Reformation in the nation's sense, was the indefensible and inalienable right of the nation itself. Out of the very heart and life of that nation arose the Renascence which finds no perfunctory record in so-called patriotic, but really dynastic history-books; yet to which the consciousness of Germany testifies, when it declares the work of Luther to have been carried on by Lessing.

To the significance of this Renascence, as to the significance of the Reformation, the House of Austria (except during the painful alternation of illusions and disappointments in Joseph II.'s reign) remained blind. But every moral and intellectual movement is an historical, and therefore a political force as well; and if it be not welcomed as a friend, it must become an adversary. The support which this movement had to bestow passed to the side of Austria's opponents, and helped to consummate the triumphs of one who only unconsciously used it—of Frederick the Great. Its historical influence has in our own day helped to drive the House of Austria out of Germany.

I say its historical influence; for of its living influence, I prefer to be absolutely silent. · But of this I am assured: that no dynasty which fails to appreciate, and itself to become instinct with the spirit of the nation, will ever permanently hold that Imperial authority which, at the most critical period of her annals, was misused and forfeited by the House of Austria.

THE HOUSE OF HABSBURG

FROM MAXIMILIAN I. TO FERDINAND III.

FERDINAND of Aragon *m.* ISABELLA of Castile.

MAXIMILIAN I. *m.* (1) MARIA of Burgundy. (2) BIANCA MARIA of Milan.

LADISLAUS II. King of Bohemia and Hungary.

JOANNA *m.* PHILIP (the Fair).

ANNA *m.* FERDINAND I.

LEWIS II. *m.* MARIA of Austria.

ELEANOR. CHARLES V.

FERDINAND I. *m.* ANNA of Bohemia and Hungary.

MARIA *m.* LEWIS II. of Hungary.

PHILIP II. MARIA.

MAXIMILIAN II. *m.* MARIA of Spain.

FERDINAND.

CHARLES *m.* MARIA of Bavaria.

DON PHILIP III. CLARA ISABELLA *m.* ALBERT of Austria. CARLOS.

RHODOLPH II. MATTHIAS. ERNEST. MAXIMILIAN. ALBERT *m.* CLARA ISABELLA of Spain.

PHILIP IV. MARIA ANNA *m.* FERDINAND III.

FERDINAND II. *m.* MARIA ANNA of Bavaria.

FERDINAND III. *m.* MARIA ANNA of Spain.

G

NOTES AND ILLUSTRATIONS.

LECTURE I.

(1) P. 3.—I doubt whether any notice has appeared in an English journal of a sufficiently remarkable lecture delivered before the Association for the History of Berlin, in October 1867, and published for a charitable purpose in the following year. The author, Per Magnus of Stockholm, takes the orthodox view of the character and career of Gustavus Adolphus; denies that his aspirations were directed towards the Imperial crown, and asserts that his life was sacrificed for religion and for the German Protestants. Deriding the "fruitless labours of a few historians of the day to tear from Gustavus Adolphus his dearly-purchased laurels," he appeals to the words spoken by King William of Prussia, when, on the 22d of September, 1865, at the monument of the Swedish king at Lützen, he was presented with a laurel wreath by a Protestant ecclesiastical dignitary. King William appears, however, to have confined himself to observations on "the enduring conflict which religion has to maintain" against "certain opponents who are endeavouring to undermine the foundation on which everything rests;" and therefore personally to consider the conditions of the struggle which he is to carry on as materially altered. And at the ceremony of the uncovering of Luther's statue at Worms, in June 1868, he seems to have maintained a discreet silence. So at least I judge from the conspicuous absence of any royal speech from the records of the Worms festivities since published by one of their managers, Dr. Eich, who is unlikely to have committed any sin of omission in a compilation which includes an infinitude of sermons, speeches, and "toasts," not to mention the telegram of her Majesty Queen Victoria, and a copy of sapphics

by Professor Nobbe, of Ciceronian fame, and, in his own words, " Lutheridarum superstitum subsenior."

(²) P. 4.—" All the wars carried on in Europe have been mixed up together, and have become *one*." (Gustavus Adolphus to Axel Oxenstjerna, 1 April, 1628. See Geijer, *Gesch. von Schweden*, vol. iii. p. 150.)

(³) P. 5.—Of this period a full and clear account, from the point of view referred to in the text, is to be found in the second volume of Droysen's *Geschichte der preussischen Politik*. Frederick III.'s reign lasted from 1439 to 1493; at its close neither Poland nor Hungary were any longer in allegiance to the Empire; and both the Arelat and Switzerland had practically passed out of its control. Against these losses and the reduction of the Imperial power to an utter nullity within the limits where it was still acknowledged, Frederick was contented to set the success of his schemes for securing the Burgundian heritage to his house. The desire for reform expressed itself with particular eagerness during the years 1454-7, at a time when the Emperor, while declaring his submission to Pope Calixtus, thus described the condition of the German nation : " On all sides our enemies are upon us, while we are turning our arms against ourselves; righteously we suffer for our guilt : amongst us there is no union, no obedience; we submit neither to the spiritual nor to the temporal head; religion is contemned, justice lies low, fidelity is almost unknown; each deems himself to be king and pope: as many heads, so many opinions; the people is torn asunder by conflicting interests; a thousand feuds undermine Germany." And later, in 1471, at the Diet of Ratisbon (where there had been actually talk of deposing the " useless " Emperor), renewed attempts were made at Imperial reform; yet Frederick was able to extricate himself by private concessions to the princes, and by illusory emendations in the judicial system of the Empire. When I speak of his " cynical apathy," I refer to the feature in his character illustrated by Ranke (*Deutsche Geschichte im Zeitalter der Reformation*, i. 95) with such anecdotes as the following: "When the cities and princes, armed for war in 1449, rejected his mediation, he resolved to let well alone. He would wait, he said, till they had mutually burnt down their houses and devastated their corn-fields ; after that, they would of a certainty come and request him to reconcile them with one another ; and thus it shortly came to pass."

The revival of the Papal power may of course be dated from the healing of the Schism in 1447. By the year 1460, Pope Pius II. (the Æneas Silvius whose diplomacy had put an end to the Council of Basel) could declare all appeals to a Council deserving of condemnation; and, by the commencement of the next century, a Dominican publicist could declare the Church a born slave, who in the case of a bad Pope could do nothing further than persistently pray against him—the *precibus et lacrymis* theory which King James I. afterwards applied to the relations between a king and his subjects. (Ranke, *u. s.* p. 238.)

(⁴) P. 5.—At Frankfort, at the time of Maximilian's election as Roman king in 1485, a Jew was said to have prophesied that this was the last German prince who would ever be chosen for the office. (Droysen, ii. 353.) Charles V., as is well known, never learnt to speak German perfectly. The view which I take of Maximilian's general policy is in substance that brought out with incomparable force in Sybel's classic essay, *Die deutsche Nation und das Kaiserreich.* The two Eastern matrimonial alliances were those between one of Maximilian's grandsons and Anna, the daughter of Ladislaus, King of Bohemia and Hungary (and brother of Sigismund, King of Poland); and between Ladislaus' son Lewis, and Maximilian's grand-daughter Maria. These engagements, contracted in 1515, were fulfilled in 1520. (Mailath, *Gesch. Oesterreichs,* i. 384.) The price paid for them was the confirmation of the "perpetual peace" of Thorn (of 1466), by which Prussia was placed in vassalage to the crown of Poland. This act declared the desertion of the German Order by the Emperor, who had bidden it confide in his protection. (See Treitzschke, *Das deutsche Ordensland Preussen,* in *Hist. und Polit. Aufsätze,* p. 59.) Maximilian's last Diet was that of Augsburg, in 1518. The saying that "the money for the war against the Turks was intended for the pockets of the Roman courtiers," was Ulrich von Hutten's; and Luther refers in September of the same year to information from Rome as "Romanæ astutiæ, de decimis novis exigendis, pro bello adversus Turcas, quæ evidenter excogitatæ a Florentinis, avarissimis omnium quos cœlum tegit, cognoscuntur. Ipsi enim Pontificis facilitate utuntur in omnem suæ voraginis libidinem." (See R. Rössler, *Die Kaiserwahl Karl's V.,* p. 37, note.) · The notion of Maximilian I. as "the first German landsknecht" will not seem strange to the readers of Mr. Brewer's account of the transactions in connexion with the Holy League of 1510, according to which Maximilian was to receive 200,000 gold crowns for making himself generally useful in attacking the extra-Italian dominions of Lewis XII. (*Letters and Papers, &c. of the Reign of Henry VIII.* vol. i. Preface, pp. xxxvii. ff.); and specially to the picture of Maximilian, at the siege of Terouenne, taking service under Henry as one of his captains for the pay of 100 crowns a day, which Queen Katharine very naturally designated "the greatest honour that ever came to prince." (Kath. to Wolsey, Ellis's *Original Letters*, vol. i. p. 85. See also Sharon Turner's *History of the Reign of Henry VIII.* vol. i. p. 120.) For a typical enthusiasm, wide enough to include both Maximilian and his "Landsknechte," see the industrious monograph by Barthold, *George von Frundsberg und das deutsche Kriegshandwerk, z. z. d. Reformation,* where the true explanation of the term "Landsknechte" is given : viz. mercenaries from the lowland country of Austria, as opposed to those from the Swiss mountains. And, to give only one instance of the mythical Maximilian of modern German poetry, see the intrinsically charming "wreath of romances," entitled *Der letzte Ritter,* by Anastasias Grün (Count Auersperg.) The quotation at the close of the paragraph is from "Ain newes lied von Kunig Karolus," printed in Liliencron's *Historische Volkslieder der Deutschen,* &c. vol. iii. pp. 229–231.

(⁵) P. 7.—The so-called "Imperial matricula of Worms" (according to which the levy of a certain number of troops at a certain rate of pay was imposed upon the several estates of the realm) of the year 1521, remained the basis of the financial system of the Empire till its dissolution in 1805 ; the so-called "Usual-matriculæ" of 1698 and 1737 never having come into general use. (See Hermann Schulze, *Einleitung in das deutsche Staatsrecht,* p. 260.) Thus it is obvious that there is some progress in human affairs; for Count Bismarck has only calculated the *matricula* of his Federal State for four years, whereas the old Germanic Confederation retained its original calculation for fifty, and the Empire had retained *its* scale for nearly three centuries.

(⁶) P. 8.—Professor Maurenbrecher, at the close of his most valuable work *Karl V. und die deutschen Protestanten,* which contains a clear representation, based chiefly upon hitherto unpublished documents from the archives of Simancas, of the conflict between Charles V.

and the Reformation, and its connexion with the general progress of events in Europe. The following passage (pp. 171-2) seems to me to contain the kernel of the question as to the relation between the political ideal and the religious views of the great Emperor :—

" He had become persuaded by the feeling that he was an Emperor, such as the great Emperors of the Middle Ages had been. His due, so he deemed, was not only the first rank in Christendom, but simply the dominion and supremacy over all the other lands of Europe. Thus the other kings were not in his eyes endowed with equal rights to his own ; on the contrary, he regarded himself as their ordained master. The German Princes, of course, he could only treat like Spanish grandees ; nor could he ever comprehend the peculiar nature of his German sovereignty.

" And yet this lord of the West, notwithstanding all the political tendencies and aims which he pursued on all sides in order to extend his power over the other countries of Europe, was at the same time, at the very bottom of his soul, possessed by the religiosity of his native Spain. In him we recognise a strange commingling of temporal and religious ideas. It is to judge the Emperor ill, to see in him merely the conqueror and the despot ; nor is the peculiarity of his character comprehended even by those who think to find in him merely the religious zealot. When this Emperor roused himself for his last great blow against France, he permitted to his son a glance into the depths of his soul. And these writings, addressed by the Emperor to his son, are all instinct with a certain feeling of melancholy, a certain feeling of resignation, which forces its way through all his pieces of political advice, and all his artifices of statecraft. He, whose task it is to repress and fight down France, perceives that at the same time the preservation of the true Church is laid on the shoulders of himself alone. Throughout all the widenings and intricacies of his statecraft, towards both Pope and Protestants, he keeps steadily before his eyes the great end : to restore the Church in her ancient glóry, and to save her in immaculate purity out of the hands of Protestantism. I believe it to be an utterly useless quarrel to attempt to discuss the question : whether in these Spanish kings—Charles V. and Philip II. alike—the ecclesiastical sentiments of their Catholicism, or the political tendency of their European position, furnished the first and decisive impulse to their course of action ; in both of them these were intimately interwoven ; their policy and their religion rest on the same basis within their minds."

And again (p. 344), in a passage referred to in the text of my lecture :

" I am thoroughly convinced of the identity of the aims of Philip and of Charles. It is one and the same idea which animated and inspired both father and son ; it is one and the same faith by which father and son were comforted in defeat, and elevated in victory. To direct Christendom at large, under the ordinances of the mediæval Church, this system of a mediæval conception was that which these Spanish rulers pursued by all the methods of the modern system of government, and with all the instruments of modern statecraft."

(7) P. 9.—The Treaty of Passau was concluded in 1552 ; Charles V. only signing it with great reluctance, and, according to one account, leaving himself an opening for its future violation by omitting to affix his seal. The religious Peace of Augsburg was concluded by King Ferdinand in 1555, Charles (who was now residing in Spain) refusing to take any part in the transaction. By "*Deutsche Libertät* " I understand that complex of the rights of the individual estate of the realm which was afterwards thus extended in the Peace of West- phalia :—" Ut autem provisum sit . . . . omnes et singuli electores, principes et status imperii Romani in antiquis suis juribus, præroga- tivis, libertate, privilegiis libero juris territorialis tam in ecclesiasticis quam politicis exercitio, ditionibus, regalibus, horumque omnium possessione, vigore hujus transactionis, ita stabiliti firmatique sunto, ut a nullo unquam sub quocunque prætextu de facto turbari possint vel debeant." For before the peace the "liberties" of an estate were comprehended within the individual rights and royalties con- ferred upon him, and by those rights belonging to all estates in common, in virtue of the usage, or of particular fundamental laws, of the Empire (*Reichsherkommen, Reichsgrundgesetze*). Among the latter are to be included the treaties of Passau and Augsburg. (Cf. Pütter, *Geist d. Westph. Friedens,* pp. 456–7 ; and H. Schulze, *u. s.* pp. 221–4.) The Augsburg Treaty liberated the Protestant estates from the episcopal jurisdiction within their territories. Henry II. of France, in his manifesto of 1551, declared himself on the title-page, "vindex libertatis Germanicæ," and in the text declared that the complaints "of many princes and other worthy persons of the German nation," left no doubt on his mind but that

"the Emperor and the House of Austria, to the eternal ruin of German national liberty, were about to establish an absolute monarchy." In 1552 he occupied Verdun, Toul, and Metz; and retained them after Maurice and his allies had made their peace with the Emperor at Passau. (See Adolf Schmidt, *Elsass und Lothringen.*)

(8) P. 11.—Briefly stated, the *reservatum ecclesiasticum* provided that in the case of the conversion of a spiritual Estate to the Augsburg (Lutheran) Confession, that Estate should *eo ipso* forfeit all his spiritual dignities and their concomitant emoluments. The Protestants had left the question as to the insertion of this clause to the arbitrament of Ferdinand; he decided in its favour; but the Protestants, though they swore to the treaty, refused to acknowledge the reservation as binding upon them. The Jesuit "opinion" was obtained by the Pope through the General of the Order, Borgia, in 1566; one of the three Jesuits who drew it up was Canisius. (See Ritter, *Gesch. der deutschen Union*, vol. i. p. 6.) The family compact referred to is that of Augsburg, by which it was agreed (in March 1551) that Ferdinand should succeed Charles as Emperor, and himself be succeeded by Philip, who in his turn should be followed by Ferdinand's son Maximilian.

(9) P. 13.—As to the early training of Maximilian II., and the details of what may fairly be called his conversion, see an essay by E. Reimann, *Die religiöse Entwicklung Max. II., in den Jahren* 1554 *bis* 1564; in Sybel's *Histor. Zeitschr.* vol. xv. (1866). The insinuation as to the ladies is made by Gindely, *Rudolf II. und seine Zeit*, vol. i. p. 24. When Maximilian declared to his father Ferdinand his determination to adhere to the Catholic faith, and to live and die in it, the Emperor, while commending this resolution, expressed his belief in its sincerity; and at the same time his conviction that, "were it otherwise, no earthly consideration would cause his son to conceal his real opinion." Hereupon Maximilian solemnly reiterated his promise. I think it will be conceded that we have here a transaction of a different nature from that which Henry of Navarre flippantly related in his famous 'Aside to Gabrielle.' (See Motley, *History of the United Netherlands*, vol. iii. p. 241.) Philippina Welser, referred to on p. 12, was the daughter of a citizen of Augsburg; and her story (not unparalleled in the annals of the House of Habsburg) has served as theme for many a German poet,

most recently for one, the grace of whose verse is only surpassed by the beauty of his prose—Paul Heyse.

([10]) P. 15.—According to Droysen (*Gesch. d. pr. Pol.* vol. ii. p. 5), the word '*Polizei*,' which in modern German signifies Police, was in the fifteenth century used in the sense of '*Politie*,' or art of government.

([11]) P. 17.—Dr. Anton Gindely, in his work *Rudolph II. u. seine Zeit* (of which the first volume was published in 1863); and in a variety of papers contributed to the Transactions of the Imperial Academy of Sciences at Vienna, during late years. To him we particularly owe the demonstration of the very gradual restoration of the political intimacy between Austria and Spain which converted the German quarrel into a European war. These publications have great value for the English historian who is willing to introduce the element of intelligibility into a view of the foreign policy of King James I. Many details concerning the personality of Rhodolph II. are derived by Gindely from the relations of the Venetian Ambassadors. The reception of Rhodolph and his brother in Spain is described by Gachard, *Don Carlos et Philippe II.*, tome i. ch. 5; and in the ninth chapter of the same volume is presented an authentic portrait of the Spanish king at the time when his personality would naturally exercise the strongest influence upon his nephews.—The story of Katharine and Isabella is told by Prescott, *History of the Reign of Philip II.*, bk. iv. c. 8.—As to the son of William the Silent, whom the Spaniards "kidnapped and Hispaniolised," see Motley, *History of the United Netherlands*, vol. iii. pp. 354, 355, *et al.*

([12]) P. 21.—For a full account of the extraordinary career of this individual, see F. Hurter's monograph, *Philipp Lang, Kammerdiener Kaiser Rudolph's II.* Lang was a Jew, which M. Hurter seems somehow to regard as an aggravation of his offences. The value of his possessions, at the time when a stop was at last put upon his proceedings, was estimated at 300,000 florins, besides much upon which it was impossible to lay hands. Lang was in 1609 sentenced on several counts to death, and on others to perpetual incarceration; and he appears to have died in prison (where a servant was allowed him) early in 1610. His wife obtained a decent annuity from the Emperor Matthias!

([13]) P. 21.—Daniel Eremita, whose journal well deserves republication, was attached to an embassy sent, in 1609, by the Grand-Duke of Tuscany to the Emperor Rhodolph II., and several princes of the Empire. They waited upon the Emperor at Prague, upon the Elector (Christian II.) of Saxony at Torgau, upon the Elector (Joachim II.) of Brandenburg at Berlin ; upon the Margrave of Brandenburg-Anspach, the Landgrave of Hesse, the Prince of Anhalt-Dessau, the spiritual electors of Trèves and Mayence, the Bishop of Würzburg, the Duke of Württenburg, Philip Lewis Count Palatine at Neuburg, and the authorities of the Free Imperial cities of Ulm, Nürnberg and Augsburg. Brunswick they avoided on account of the plague prevailing there ; and Frederick IV, Elector Palatine, was unable to receive them at Heidelberg, being laid up with the gout. Daniel Eremita is a shrewd observer, fully conscious of his superiority as an Italian and a Catholic, and by no means dazzled by the splendour which the German courts exhibited. His journal leaves the impression that (as in the succeeding century) the highest degree of culture was to be found at the courts of the Spiritual Electors, and in the Free Cities. The memorials close with an enthusiastic description of the wonderful clock at Augsburg— "quod sane ut omnium operum et artium complementum et finis, ita finis epistolæ meæ erit ;" for the age shared Rhodolph II.'s love of mechanical inventions, and the Italian traveller would have been shocked to be obliged to confess (like Yorick on contemplating the "great clock of Lippius of Basil," at Lyons), that he could hardly account for the great devotion with which he beheld its "surprising movements."

(14) P. 23.—A full account of these transactions is given by Gindely, *u.s.* The Capuchin friar was the well-known Lawrence of Brindisi. When John Frederick, the brother of Bernard of Weimar, was confined in consequence of his dangerous mania, his brothers similarly approached him through a clerical medium. (B. Röse, *Johann Friedrich VI. H. zu Sachsen,* p. 101.) No history of the Thirty Years' War should fail to take into account the operation of the belief in dæmonology, then so prevalent both in court and camp. See, among recent publications on this topic, C. Schneider, *Der allgemeine und der Krieger-Aberglaube im* 16., 17., *u.* 18. *Jahrh.*— Rhodolph proposed to marry a Tuscan princess. (Ritter, *Gesch. d. d. Union,* vol. i. p. 249.)

(15) P. 24.—Ludwig Häusser, *Gesch. d. Zeitalters d. Reformation,*

(published posthumously from the lectures of the lamented historian), p. 487.

([16]) P. 26.—Quoted by Hurter (*Gesch. Ferdinand's II. u. seiner Eltern*, vol. iii. p. 412, note): "Laurati in agro Piceno coram Virgine Matri Deo vovit, vel cum vitæ discrimine abacturum se e Styria, Carinthia, Carniòla sectas sectarumque magistros." Of course the story grew, as Hurter indignantly points out, while he confirms the authenticity of its germ.

([17]) P. 28.—The Jesuits were introduced into Styria in 1572; the two first of the order coming not from Bavaria, but from the Tyrol. (See Hurter, *u.s.* vol. i. p. 260, note.) The allusion on p. 27 is to Droysen's *Testament d. grossen Kurfürsten*. I need hardly say with how much hesitation I venture to differ from any conclusions arrived at by one of the master historians of this generation ; but I confess that, after all the perversions have been removed by him from the consideration of the question, the fact seems to me to remain that the great Elector before his death disintegrated the dominion which he had been accumulating—for the benefit of an historical theory of the future.

([18]) P. 30.—The University of Ingolstadt stood at this period at the height of its fame. According to Schreiber, *Maximilian I. d. Kathol.* pp. 6, 7, it was attended by students of all classes, from the prince to the poor man's son, and of various countries—Poland, Italy, Spain, France, Belgium, Denmark, and England. Even Protestants were attracted by its reputation. Among its teachers were the English physician, Edmund Holling, and "Robert Turner, of Devonshire, to whom, expatriated by the intolerance of Queen Elizabeth, Ingolstadt offered a learned asylum." As to the reputation of Eck, see Ranke, *Deutsche Geschichte*, &c., vol. i. pp. 399–401. He had begun to lecture at Ingolstadt in his twentieth year. The University of Wittenberg was founded by Frederick the Wise, in 1502. As to the Electress Magdalena Sibylla see Koch, *Gesch. d. deutsch. Reiches unter Ferd. III.* vol. i. p. 5. On hearing the report of the death of the Elector of Bavaria, she expressed a hope that the Emperor and Tilly might meet with a similar fate, in which case she would "don a robe of variegated hue instead of a suit of sables." The religious views of this sagacious princess did not prevent her from penetrating the worldly motives of the court-preacher, Hoë von Hoënegg. (See Müller, *Joh. Georg. u. sein Hof*, p. 198)

(¹⁹) P. 31.—Maximilian I.'s '*Monita Paterna*' were first published in Adlzreitter's *Annales Boicæ gentis;* after which several translations from the original Latin appeared in different modern languages. The edition from which I quote is that of Aretin (1822), which accompanies the Latin text by a German parallel version. Aretin gives a curious list of similar works by royal hands, from Constantius to the unfortunate Gustavus III. of Sweden. As to Ferdinand's motto, taken from 2 Timothy ii. 5, see Hurter, *u.s.* vol. ii. p. 235 and note. I have not thought it necessary to mention a quarrel about precedence between Ferdinand and Maximilian, which much occupies their several biographers.

(²⁰) P. 32.—For an account of the training of the Weimar princes, under the eye of their admirable mother Dorothea Maria, see the first volume of Röse's *Herzog Bernhard d. Grosse von Sachsen-Weimar.* She had borne her lord eleven sons, of whom Bernard was the youngest. Of these eleven, seven arrived at man's estate ; and while the eldest remained at home to administer the paternal inheritance, six went out to do battle for the cause of Protestantism and princely "liberty ;" and three died in the field. The readers of Schiller will not forget his eloquent apostrophe to the unfortunate John Frederick, the victim of Mühlberg, as avenged by his heroic descendants. (*Dreissigj. Krieg*, I. Buch.) Unhappily, Bernard avenged John Frederick by the policy of Maurice.

(²¹) P. 34.—Both these lines of defence seem to me to be adopted by Hurter in his chapter on the "execution of the ecclesiastical restoration," *u.s.* vol. iv. p. 218, ff.

(²²) P. 34.—The following account of this *coup d'état*, as he calls it, is quoted by Müller, *Fünf Bücher vom Böhmischen Kriege*, p. 33, from a letter written by the Saxon envoy at Vienna :—"Yesterday afternoon about two o'clock Cardinal Klesel was introduced by the apostolical nuncio to an audience before the Archduke Maximilian ; but when he had entered the presence-chamber, Master Seyfried Breuner, *in the name of the entire House of Austria, wherein the King in Spain was also mentioned*, arrested him prisoner; whereupon he was in the presence of certain cavaliers, among them Count Dampierre, Count Collalto, Conte Cuculi, &c., secretly led into a great apartment ; and although he vainly desired to be taken before his Imperial Majesty, and appealed to his clerical character, his request was refused, and his appeal quashed by the exhibition of a Papal bull; whereupon he (the Cardinal) was deprived of his red coat and hat, and, instead, dressed in a black hat and cloak of cloth. Thereafter, unknown to his people, he was conducted by the long narrow passage by the city wall to the other bastion, placed in the carriage there held in readiness, and taken by Breuner in a closed carriage to the *Neustadt*, and, it is said, to the Tyrol. All his gear was sealed up, and an inventory thereof taken this day in presence of Count Mansfeld and the Chief Chamberlain; and his servants, with the reverend Prior, were placed under arrest. Ferdinand, Maximilian, and the Spanish Ambassador have hereupon notified this to the Emperor; and on the following day to the Empress also. For the rest, his Imperial Majesty has of late, and up to yesterday, been in good health and spirits (*ist itzo, und noch gestern, wohlauf gewesen*)."

(23) P. 35.—According to the Golden Bull of Charles IV., the Bohemian crown was undoubtedly elective; but Ferdinand I. had in 1545 declared it hereditary; and the declaration had been practically acquiesced in. Yet Matthias himself had been only *elected* successor to it in 1608, and thus the House of Austria had again waived its unwarrantable claim. The Protestant party protested against the nomination of Ferdinand (II.) as interfering with free election; but they relinquished their protest in consideration of his conciliatory attitude towards the question of their privileges; *after* he had sworn on the Scripture that he would maintain them, and after he had undertaken to abstain from interference during the reign of Matthias. These were the promises which he broke.

(24) P. 36.—In order that there might be no mistake as to the exclusion of the Calvinists from this Lutheran jubilee, the court-preacher, Hoë von Hoënegg (see Note 30), "analysed" the text given out for the sermons to be preached on the occasion for the benefit of the ordinary clerical mind. (See Böttiger, *Gesch. Sachsens*, vol. ii. p. 54.)

(25) P. 39.—I have no wish, in a mere note, to pursue a question of so transcendent an historical importance. But, leaving Leo X. out of the question, I beg the reader's consideration of the character and antecedents of Adrian VI., and of the actual proceedings in the direction of a "rational Papacy," favoured by Paul III. (see Ranke's *Popes*, bk. i. chap. 3; and bk. ii.). The "critical moment" to which I refer was that when Luther accepted and met the mediation

of Miltitz, which the unfortunate activity of Eck and the zeal of the Dominicans were allowed to render futile. That opportunity was irreparably lost after the Leipzig Disputation; and thus it has come to pass that, in the solemn words of a Cardinal of the Roman Church (Diepenbrock), it is the duty of German Catholics, till the day of reconciliation dawns, to bear the schism of the faith "in the spirit of repentance for a common guilt." These words are quoted by Döllinger in the memorable introduction to his book on the Church and the Churches (*Kirche und Kirchen*, Munich, 1861), where that great and generous theologian has thus spoken in his own name : "We must acknowledge, that in this instance also God has permitted much good, by the side of much evil, to issue out of the errors of men, out of the conflicts and passions of the sixteenth century ; that the impulse of the German nation, towards the abolition of those abuses and vexations in the Church which had become intolerable, was in itself well justified, and had originated in the better qualities of our people, in its moral disgust at the mutilation and desecration of sacred things, by the abuse of religious institution for the purposes of avarice and hypocrisy. We are ready to confess that the great schism, and the agitations and troubles connected therewith, constituted a solemn judgment upon Catholic Christendom, and a judgment, too well deserved by clergy and laity, —a judgment, moreover whose effects have been salutary and purifying. The great spiritual struggle has purged the European atmosphere, has impelled the mind of mankind into new courses, and has produced a wealth of scientific and intellectual life."

H

LECTURE II.

(²⁶) P. 42.—This saying was reported to his masters, the States-General, by the envoy Francis von Ærssen, in a despatch of July 29th, 1609. (See Cornelius, *Der grosse Plan Heinrichs IV. von Frankreich*, in *Münchner Histor. Jahrbuch* for 1866.) In this very remarkable essay it is demonstrated that the supposition of the famous scheme of Henry IV. rests on the doubtful evidence of Sully's Memoirs; and that, accordingly, the current view on the subject should at least be received with cautious hesitation. The Treaty of Hall was concluded in the year 1610, shortly before the death of Henry IV. ; and, in consequence of it, the forces of the Union occupied the Duchies of Juliers, Cleves, and Berg, on behalf of the two Protestant claimants, Brandenburg and Neuburg.

(²⁷) P. 44.—For a more detailed account of the situation, see G. Droysen, *Gustav Adolf*, vol. i. bk. ii., where the attitude of Denmark is fully explained.

(²⁸) P. 44.—I confess that I am unable to discover the authority for the famous anecdote referred to in the text. Khevenhiller, *Annales Ferdinandei*, tom. ix. p. 398, is too decorous to enter into the particulars of the conduct of Thonrädel and the other members of this determined deputation, though he mentions Dampierre's 500 cuirassiers as "*miraculose*" appearing at the critical moment. The story is repeated by Häusser, *u. s.* p. 495, where the words are given, " Nandel, surrender ; thou must subscribe !" The familiar diminutive constitutes no addition to the insult ; for the Viennese have always treated the Imperial house as their domestic property ; and we find Ferdinand's mother, in her correspondence, speaking of her daughter Anna (afterwards Queen of Poland) as "Andl." The first Emperor of Austria was allowed to hide many sins of omission and commission under the aspect of "a good Viennese" (cf. Springer, *Gesch. Oesterreichs*, vol. i. p. 111). The ceremonies at the coronation of Ferdinand II. are described in a pamphlet of the year 1619, where the sword of Charlemagne and the simultaneous imposition of the crown by "all the three spiritual electors," are mentioned with particular emphasis.

(29) P.45.—The refusal of Frederick the Wise to accept the proffered support of a majority of the electors was founded upon considerations not dissimilar to those which may have prompted the rumoured "*Pas si bête*" of King Ferdinand of Portugal. (See R. Rössler, *Die Kaiserwahl Karl's V.* p. 193.) Rössler refers to *Spalatin's Nachlass*, p. 59, where the reader will find a very enthusiastic account of the discretion and firmness manifested on this occasion by Spalatin's master.

(30) P. 49.—As to the earlier projects of the Bavarian line to secure the Palatinate Electorate, see Kluckhohn, *Briefe Friedrich d. Frommen v. d. Pfalz*, vol. i. p. 45. Daniel Eremita's description of Christian II. commences thus :—"Hujus tibi formam describere pæne pudori duco. Nihil in illo, quo Principem cognoscas. Immanis bellua ; voce, auribus, omni corporis gestu convenienti destituta. Nutu tantum et concrepitis digitorum articulis loquitur ; nec inter familiares quidem, nisi obscœna quædam, et fere per convicium, jactat. In vultu ejus nihil placidum ; rubor et maculæ, e vino contractæ, oris lineamenta confuderant. Vasta corporis forma, proceri et immensi artus, sed inconditi. Vestis nullo cultu, sed detrita, et sordibus obsita. Atque, ut in breve omnia contraham, nomine tenus Princeps est." This amiable and accomplished prince died in June 1611, from the consequences of what the Saxon historian, Böttiger, calls "a too rapid potation." John George I., who succeeded him, reigned till 1656. Ample opportunities are afforded by the researches of Karl August Müller (*Kurfürst Johann Georg I., seine Familie, und sein Hof*) for arriving at a conclusion as to the private character, as well as to the system of government in his state, of this Elector. His conduct with respect to the war will, of course, be variously judged. It was guided by dynastic considerations ; but he was faithful to the Emperor as long as the latter adhered to the engagements which he had contracted towards Saxony. The Albertine line of the House of Wettin is not to be branded with infamy, because of the

double treason of the founder of its greatness, or because of the sins of Augustus 'the physically strong.' It has numbered many princes whose patriotism and good faith have dignified misfortune; and many who have, to the extent of their ability, contributed to make Saxony what it is—the very heart of Germany.—To Hoë von Hoënegg reference has been already made; his influence was exerted throughout the first half of the war against the Calvinists; and in favour of the House of Austria, which encouraged him by presents of Peruvian gold. (Gfrörer, *Gustav Adolf*, p. 603.) In the song from which I have quoted (it forms one of Opel and Cohn's interesting collection), Pater Job (a representative of the Catholic priests), Herr Matz (Hoënegg), and Father Abraham (Scultetus, the spiritual adviser of Frederick, Elector Palatine) are held up to popular odium as the real authors of the existing misery:—

> "God, left alone, would set things right;
> It is the priests who cause the blight."

(O. u. C., *Der dreissigjährige Krieg*, p. 105.)   Schwarzenberg's policy has met with elaborate attempts at defence as well as assaults; into the merits of which it is impossible here to enter. And I hope to find another occasion for discussing the difficult question as to the reasons of Gustavus Adolphus' delay in coming to the rescue of Magdeburg, which, notwithstanding the insinuations of such writers as Klopp, and his echo Keym, I believe to have been truly stated in the Swedish king's own Apology.—The name of Joachim II.'s Jew was Lippold.—Already at the time of the *Interim*, Magdeburg was, in Protestant Germany, saluted as the " chancery of God."

([31]) P. 51.—Müller, *Böhmischer Krieg*, p. 308. My view of the conduct of King James is founded upon a consideration of Mr. S. R.'Gardiner's *Letters, &c.*, *illustrating the Relations between England and Germany at the Commencement of the Thirty Years' War* (printed for the Camden Society in 1865). These seem to me to prove that James was not wise *before* the event; and that he wished the event to decide the question which distracted courtiers and envoys: whether he approved, or disapproved, of Frederick's acceptance of the Bohemian crown.

([32]) P. 52.—The quotation is from Opel and Cohn, *u. s.* p. 106. Wootton's charming lines to the Princess Elizabeth are printed in Mr. Palgrave's *Golden Treasury*, p. 71. The interest which Ralegh took in the favourite sister of his Prince Henry, is evinced by his *Discourse* on the proposal of marrying her to the Prince of Piedmont (1611). But her history is naturally to English readers the most familiar episode of the great war.—The attempt at rehabilitating Tilly, already partially made by Gfrörer, was elaborately repeated in 1861 by Onno Klopp (*Tilly im dreissigjährigen Kriege*). The 'popular' historians of the same school follow in his wake ; among the rest, Keym and a patriotic annalist from whom I will venture to quote a sentence, not on account of its intrinsic value, but because it significantly exemplifies the way in which history is taught "to young and old," in districts where, as the phrase is, religious feeling runs high. "Of these two generals [Tilly and Wallenstein], the former combined the best of hearts and an *immaculate conduct* [author's italics], with the strictest military attention to duty ; while the latter obscured his gifts as a commander by an unbounded ambition and an ambiguous character ; wherefore the Emperor found himself obliged to depose him." (J. Bader, *Badische Landes-Geschichte, für Jung und Alt bearbeitet*. Freiburg im Breisgau, 1864. Third Edition, p. 251.)

(33) P. 53.—Müller, in point of fact, argues that the Bohemians might have obtained their ends by peaceable means, as the Silesians did, through the interposition of Saxony. But it remains unproved that this interposition would have been made, or, if made, accepted. The same historian, I should add, has no belief in the existence, in Ferdinand's mind, of a crusade against Protestantism ; but he proves the existence of such a plan in what he calls the "purely Jesuitico-Romanist" party, and concedes their influence upon the conduct of affairs. The passage in the *Vie de César* to which I have ventured to allude occurs tom. i. p. 339, where the argument seems to be that Cicero's *coup d'état* in suppressing the Catilinarian conspiracy was illegitimate as well as illegal : because he was not supported by the mass of the nation, and because, as representing a government which was only a faction in the state, he exposed it to the awkward charge of having saved the commonwealth for the sake of a party.

(34) P. 54.—For a full account of them see F. Kurz's *Beiträge und Geschichte d. Landes Oesterreich ob der Enns*. The author is a Catholic priest and a loyal Austrian, and is therefore unlikely to have overstated the case against the monarch whom he calls "the

good Emperor Ferdinand ;" or against the ally whom he terms the Emperor's "dear Maximilian." The Catholic historian Gfrörer, in his account of the Bohemian "judgment," is obliged to resort, in defence of Ferdinand, to a *tu quoque* against England's treatment of Ireland. Would that he had been unable to adopt even this unsatisfactory expedient !

(35) P.55.—"Clericorum Attila," in the strange doggrel in honour of the hero of the *Acta Mansfeldica*, in Opel and Cohn, *u. s.* pp. 174—179. It is strange that even Mansfeld should have met with apologists. Christian of Anhalt, as Gindely has shown, was the real author of the Union. I have before me the list of his sins in the *Copia Kaiserlicher Achtserklärung* issued against him and others in 1621. Mansfeld, after being driven by Wallenstein out of the Empire, finally set out for Venice, and died on the way, full of schemes against the victorious Emperor; but Christian made his submission, and was pardoned in 1624. In a curious little book, from which many details are to be gathered as to the court and administration of the Empire under Ferdinand II. (*Status Imp. Reg. Ferd. II.*), it is related that no sooner had the penitent been re-invested with his rights and royalties than he demanded to be allowed to cover his head in the presence; which trait of self-assurance struck the Emperor with such admiration that he not only gave the required permission, but bade Christian take a seat at the Imperial table. Christian died in 1630.

(36) P. 56.—For an account of these transactions and the proofs of the fatal influence of James I.'s balancing policy upon their progress, see G. Droysen, *Gustav Adolf*, vol. i. p. 157, f. Lord Digby was sent to Spain to make preliminary inquiries concerning the feasibility of the marriage as early as 1617 ; the journey of Charles and Buckingham to Madrid was made in the spring of 1623 ; and they were summoned home in the autumn of the same year. (See Guizot, *Un Projet de Mariage Royal.*) The fatal mistake of James lay not so much in the original conception of his policy, as in the obstinacy with which he adhered to it, long after the Spanish Government had evidently resumed a line of conduct in consonance with that of the German branch of the House of Habsburg.

(37) P.61.—Förtser has long since cleared the fame of Wallenstein from the grosser imputations under which malice and prejudice had made it suffer; but his life as a politician yet remains to be written.

In the most recent biography of Wallenstein, which professes on its title-page to be written " in the spirit of modern historical inquiry" (by W. von Janko), only a brief reference is made to the great Hanseatic scheme, though the important fact is mentioned (p. 38), on the authority of a letter in the Saxon archives, that Wallenstein was the first to conceive the idea of a canal uniting the Baltic and the German Ocean.   As to Wallenstein's share in the scheme there can be no doubt after the narrative of Droysen, *u. s.* p. 319, ff. ; and I am convinced that it is an erroneous view to believe him to have been merely interested in it for the sake of securing Mecklenburg. (This is Gfrörer's view, *Gustav Adolf,* p. 478.) The following summary of the plan is quoted by Droysen from Khevenhiller (*Annales Ferd.* xi. 143):—" Thus the King of Spain thought to attract to himself all the maritime trade; and to make the Hanse towns, which are very powerful on the Baltic and have great store of men and vessels, devoted to him ; whereby the Hollanders and Zealanders would be much weakened, and deprived of great part of their trade and profit by sea.   Thus the Emperor had already in his power several well-situated ports in the Baltic, and Wismar among the rest; and the Duke of Friedland had already been appointed Admiral over the Baltic ; who, with the aid of the Hanse towns and the vessels which he expected from Spain and Flanders, meant to take the Sound." The scheme was already described in its true character, and the reasons shown why in the interests of the Hansa it came far too late, in Sartorius, *Gesch. d. Hanseatischen Bundes,* vol. iii. p. 78, ff. Worms (*Histoire de la Ligue Hanséatique*) appears to be ignorant of the matter, or to attach no importance to it.—The English play referred to is Henry Glapthorne's *Albertus Wallenstein* (1639— 1640) ; a most wretched piece. Its scene lies alternately at " Egers" and at the Emperor's court.   W. is an ambitious ruffian who murders his son for engaging in an intrigue with one of the Duchess's women, and has the woman hanged on the stage, in the " Spanish Tragedy" style.   His other son is married at "Egers" to Emilia, daughter of "Saxon Weimar."   W., as in Schiller, is haunted by anticipations of his fate, and seeks the repose of sleep before the murder, a page singing him to rest like Brutus's boy in "Julius Cæsar."   When interrupted by the Duchess, W., in a fit of terror, kills the page. He is murdered by Gordon, Leslie, and Butler, who are charged with his removal by the Emperor. "Newman" is a comic character

of a very gross cast. The play contains no allusion to W.'s astrological pursuits, except one metaphor, where he declares that he will
not fall like a comet "by his own fire consumed." The point of
the moral is taken out by W.'s dying exclamation, —

"I die
Not for my ambition, but my cruelty."

The "admiral sans ships" occurs in the '*New Wallensteinian
Epitaph*' in Opel and Cohn, *u. s.* p. 346. A curious bundle of
epitaphs, "ex quibus facile patebit quibus Wallensteinius amicus,
quibus hostis fuerit," will be found in cap. xii. of the '*Itinerarium
Thomæ Carvæ Tipperariensis*' (the chaplain of the Irish regiment
which furnished W.'s assassins), lately reprinted by Mr. Quaritch.
Wallenstein's saying about Stralsund, which Droysen appears to
doubt, is unhesitatingly accepted by Förster (*Wallenstein's Briefe*,
vol. i. p. 234), who merely indicates the authority of the Stralsund
protonotarius Vahl for this and a similar expression of the Duke's.
(Ibid. p. 233.) The Hanseatic "jubilate" is quoted by Droysen
(p. 348) from '*Nachklang des Hänsischen Weckers ;*' and a similar
contemporary conceit is quoted by Murr (*Wallenstein's Bildnisse*
in *Beiträge zur Gesch. W.'s*, p. 390) as inscribed, under a portrait
of W., in a book published at Upsala in 1631 :—

"Dum superat tygrim, vulpemque lupumque magistros
Bestia Waldsteinius, sanguine, dente, dolo:
Respuit hoc monstrum tellus, sed suscipit unda,
Egregius rapidis fitque natator aquis."

The "Swedish and Scottish helpmates" numbered five thousand,
and were commanded by Sir Alexander Leslie. See Mr. James
Grant's *Memoirs and Adventures of Sir John Hepburn* (commander of the Scots or "Green" Brigade under Gustavus Adolphus),
p. 48, where it is stated that the Stralsunders caused medals to be
struck in remembrance of Leslie's honour and their gratitude.

(38) P. 64.—On p. 493 of his *Gustav Adolf* (Klopp's edition) Gfrörer
regrets that "nearly all the historians of the Thirty Years' War
represent the Edict of Restitution as an act of arbitrary violence and
desire for aggrandizement on the part of the Emperor, who was in
fact forced into it." Two pages further on it is noted (without
comment) that "the fullest portion of the ecclesiastical spoils," in

certain divisions of the Empire, "was designed for the youngest son of the Emperor, Leopold William, who had been educated as a clergyman." In the circles of Upper and Lower Saxony alone, 120 abbeys, and other foundations and churches, were claimed, chiefly for the Jesuits; and the complaints of Protestant princes and other estates fill several volumes in the Saxon archives. (See Helbig, *Gustav Adolf u. d. Kurfürsten von Sachsen u. Brandenburg,* p. 1, ff.) I confess myself at a loss to understand how Gfrörer can see in the promise made at Mühlhausen in 1620, "that now and hereafter (*für jetzt und später*) the occupants of ecclesiastical property in the two Saxon circles should be in no wise vexed or deprived by force," a renunciation "not *in perpetuum,* but only till times had changed." (Gfrörer, *Gustav Adolf,* p. 246.)

(39) P. 65. — See Ranke, *Französische Geschichte,* vol. ii. p. 349, ff.

(40) P. 67. — See Otto Heyne, *Der Kurfürstentag zu Regensburg von* 1630, where the situation is thus forcibly summed up:—

" From the lowest decline, and after being already near to its fall, the Austrian power had in a few years risen to a mighty height, above all by its alliance with the Catholic League. A man of ruthless energy had then created for it in his vast army a strong support, subservient to no other interest ; he had—and in truth he may, in more than one respect, be compared to the great statesman who in those days directed the destinies of France—conceived and began to realize the idea of establishing in the Empire a monarchical government, which suppressed the independence of the estates. And in point of fact he had created for the Emperor a power in Germany, of which the world had not known the like since times long-forgotten.

"But it was precisely this which had filled the princes of the League, Ferdinand's ancient allies, with the most serious anxiety, and which had aroused in them the determination to bring about, at any cost, the overthrow of the man who now held them in terror. For years they live and act in this one intent ; and it is this which they hope to accomplish at Ratisbon.

"And as in Germany, so in the whole of Europe, the wonderful rise of Austria had provoked an opposition, powerful in itself. When the meeting of the Electors opened, all the neighbours of the Emperor confronted him with open hostility or with ill-concealed aversion. And in France all found their most important reserve ;

France was, above all, the prop offering itself to the Liguistic princes, should they resolve to abandon the alliance which they had hitherto maintained with the Emperor.

"But Ferdinand appeared blind to the dangers arising against him; and, full of lofty schemes, he opened the assembly. He hoped to preserve for himself Wallenstein and his army, without at the same time giving up the Electors; rather, the latter were to support him in the execution of the aggressive plans of his foreign policy. And in addition he meant to obtain for his son the crown of Roman king; and thus to confirm in the possession of his House the Imperial power in the extent which it had reached under himself.

"How very different was the turn which events actually took! What sacrifices had not Ferdinand to make, in order to preserve to himself the Catholic princes, which he deemed himself unable to spare!

"He let drop the General, before whom the Empire trembled; he made the most important reductions in the army which constituted the principal means of power in that General's hands; with France he concluded a peace, which severed his policy from that of the other branch of the House of Habsburg, and by which he abandoned the conquests made by his victorious army; all his warlike intentions against Holland he relinquished; the election of Roman king he was unable to carry through. And in return for all this he gained nothing but aid against Sweden.

"The meeting ended with a complete victory of the Catholic League, which kept up an understanding with the Franco-Italian opposition, over the Emperor.

"But, however high a price Ferdinand had to pay, at all events the result was the continuance of the alliance, so much shaken, between the Catholic powers of the Empire. And necessarily the Protestants recognised herein an extreme danger for themselves; for against them the harmony of opposition had never been broken, and they had nowhere been able to insist upon a regard being paid to their interests. Nothing had been done to secure them by honest concessions against the origin of the Swedish war.

"And it was for this reason that Saxony and Brandenburg were induced to seek a support for themselves elsewhere. They resolved to enter into communications with the other Evangelical estates; and soon the progress of affairs led them on from this step to that of their alliance with Sweden—with the foe of Ferdinand and of the Catholic League."

(41) P. 69.—It would carry me beyond the limits of a note, were I to attempt to develop the reasons on which I ground my view of the conduct of the German war by Gustavus Adolphus. Though, on referring to Archbishop Trench's eloquent lecture on *Gustavus Adolphus* (p. 42), I observed that the natural illustration of the case of Hannibal had been employed by his Grace as well as myself, I thought it unnecessary to strike out the passage in my text; particularly as the Archbishop finds the resemblance between Hannibal and the Swedish king's motives in the improbability that either could have taken the enemy's capital had he attacked it. On this point I venture to entertain the very opposite opinion ; on the other hand, I believe that it suited neither Hannibal's nor Gustavus' plan to enter into possession of the hostile capital. The Archbishop's view of the character of Gustavus Adolphus is full of sweetness ; but the attempt which I have made for myself to understand the King's proceedings makes me consider a modification of the picture necessary in more points than one. The *Swedish Intelligencer* is the well-known chronicle of the war, of which the first part commenced with an account of the Diet of Ratisbon. The exclusion of Gustavus Adolphus' agent from the Lübeck conferences was undoubtedly anticipated by the King ; although the attempts of the envoy (Salvius) to obtain a hearing are almost unsurpassed in the history of diplomacy. A full account of them was given by the envoy's secretary Lehausen, to the Frenchman Ogier, when the latter visited Stockholm in the suite of the French embassy in 1634. (See Ogerii *Ephemerides*. Paris, 1656.) The object of Gustavus Adolphus was obviously to be insulted ; and Salvius individually obtained his revenge, inasmuch as he lived to be one of the Swedish plenipotentiaries at the negotiations for the Peace of Westphalia.

(42) P. 73.—The best recent work on the reign of Ferdinand III. is that of M. Koch (*Geschichte des deutschen Reiches unter der Regierung Ferd. III.*), of which two volumes have been published. The second reaches up to the Peace of Westphalia, and thus concludes the survey of the policy of the House of Austria during the war. It is written in a friendly spirit towards that House ; and thus the question as to the altered relations between it and the Jesuits is, perhaps, hardly treated with the requisite incisiveness. The

Alice's Adventures in Wonderland.
> By LEWIS CARROLL. With Forty-two Illustrations by TENNIEL. 14th Thousand. Crown 8vo. cloth. **6s.**

ALLINGHAM.—*Laurence Bloomfield in Ireland.*
> A Modern Poem. By WILLIAM ALLINGHAM. Fcap. 8vo. **7s.**

ANSTED.—*The Great Stone Book of Nature.*
> By DAVID THOMAS ANSTED, M.A. F.R.S. F.G.S. Fcap. 8vo. **5s.**

ANSTIE.—*Stimulants and Narcotics, their Mutual Relations.*
> With Special Researches on the Action of Alcohol, Æther, and Chloroform on the Vital Organism. By FRANCIS E. ANSTIE, M.D. M.R.C.P. 8vo. **14s.**

Neuralgia, and Diseases which resemble it.
> 8vo. [In the Press.

Aristotle on Fallacies ; or, the Sophistici Elenchi.
> With a Translation and Notes by EDWARD POSTE, M.A. 8vo. **8s. 6d.**

ARNOLD.—*Works by* MATTHEW ARNOLD.
> *New Poems. Second Edition.*
> > Extra fcap. 8vo. **6s. 6d.**

> *A French Eton ; or, Middle-Class Education and the State.*
> > Fcap. 8vo. **2s. 6d.**

> *Essays in Criticism.*
> > *New Edition.* Extra fcap. 8vo. **6s.**

> *Schools and Universities on the Continent.*
> > 8vo. **10s. 6d.**

BAKER.—*Works by* SIR SAMUEL W. BAKER, M.A. F.R.G.S.
> *The Nile Tributaries of Abyssinia, and the Sword Hunters of the Hamran Arabs.*
> > With Portraits, Maps, and Illustrations. *Third Edition.* 8vo. **21s.**

> *The Albert N'yanza Great Basin of the Nile, and Exploration of the Nile Sources. New and cheaper Edition.*
> > With Portraits, Maps, and Illustrations. Two Vols. crown 8vo. **16s.**

> *Cast up by the Sea ; or, The Adventures of Ned Grey.*
> > With Illustrations. Crown 8vo.

BARWELL.—*Guide in the Sick Room.*
> By RICHARD BARWELL, F.R.C.S. Extra fcap. 8vo. **3s. 6d.**

BARNES.—*Poems of Rural Life in Common English.*
By the Rev. W. BARNES, Author of " Poems of Rural Life in the Dorset Dialect." Fcap. 8vo. *6s.*

BATES AND LOCKYER.—*A Class-Book of Geography. Adapted to the recent programme of the Royal Geographical Society.*
By H. W. BATES and J. N. LOCKYER, F.R.G.S. [In the Press.

BAXTER.—*National Income.*
By R. DUDLEY BAXTER, M.A. With Coloured Diagram. 8vo. *3s. 6d.*

BAYMA.—*Elements of Molecular Mechanics.*
By JOSEPH BAYMA, S. J. 8vo. *10s. 6d.*

BEASLEY.—*An Elementary Treatise on Plane Trigonometry.*
With a Numerous Collection of Examples. By R. D. BEASLEY, M.A. *Second Edition.* Crown 8vo. *3s. 6d.*

BELL.—*Romances and Minor Poems.*
By HENRY GLASSFORD BELL. Fcap. 8vo. *6s.*

BERNARD.—*The Progress of Doctrine in the New Testament.*
In Eight Lectures preached before the University of Oxford. By THOMAS DEHANY BERNARD, M.A. *Second Edition.* 8vo. *8s. 6d.*

BERNARD.—*Four Lectures on Subjects connected with Diplomacy.*
By MOUNTAGUE BERNARD, M.A., Chichele Professor of International Law and Diplomacy, Oxford. 8vo. *9s.*

BERNARD (ST.).—*The Life and Times of St. Bernard, Abbot of Clairvaux.*
By J. C. MORISON, M.A. *New Edition.* Crown 8vo. *7s. 6d.*

BESANT.—*Studies in Early French Poetry.*
By WALTER BESANT, M.A. Crown 8vo. *8s. 6d.*

BIRKS.—*Works by* THOMAS RAWSON BIRKS, M.A.
The Difficulties of Belief in connexion with the Creation and the Fall.
Crown 8vo. *4s. 6d.*

On Matter and Ether ; or, the Secret Laws of Physical Change.
Crown 8vo. *5s. 6d.*

A 2

BLAKE.—*The Life of William Blake, the Artist.*
> By ALEXANDER GILCHRIST. With numerous Illustrations from Blake's Designs and Fac-similes of his Studies of the "Book of Job." Two Vols. Medium 8vo. 32s.

BLAKE.—*A Visit to some American Schools and Colleges.*
> By SOPHIA JEX BLAKE. Crown 8vo. 6s.

Blanche Lisle, and other Poems.
> By CECIL HOME. Fcap. 8vo. 4s. 6d.

BOOLE.—*Works by the late* GEORGE BOOLE, F.R.S. *Professor of Mathematics in the Queen's University, Ireland, &c.*

> *A Treatise on Differential Equations.*
> **New Edition.** Edited by I. TODHUNTER, M.A. F.R.S. Crown 8vo. 14s.

> *Treatise on Differential Equations.*
> Supplementary Volume. Crown 8vo. 8s. 6d.

> *A Treatise on the Calculus of Finite Differences.*
> Crown 8vo. 10s. 6d.

BRADSHAW.—*An Attempt to ascertain the state of Chaucer's Works, as they were Left at his Death,*
> With some Notices of their Subsequent History. By HENRY BRADSHAW, of King's College, and the University Library, Cambridge.   [In the Press.

BRIGHT.—*Speeches on various Questions of Public Policy.*
> By JOHN BRIGHT, M.P. Edited by PROFESSOR THOROLD ROGERS. 2 vols. 8vo. 25s.

BRIMLEY.—*Essays by the late* GEORGE BRIMLEY, M.A.
> Edited by W. G. CLARK, M.A. With Portrait. *Cheaper Edition.* Fcap. 8vo. 3s. 6d.

BROOK SMITH.—*Arithmetic in Theory and Practice.*
> For Advanced Pupils. Part First. By J. BROOK SMITH, M.A. Crown 8vo. 3s. 6d.

BRYCE.—*The Holy Roman Empire.*
> By JAMES BRYCE, B.C.L. Fellow of Oriel College, Oxford. *A New Edition, revised and enlarged.* Crown 8vo. 9s.

BUCKNILL.—*The Mad Folk of Shakespeare.*
> Psychological Lectures by J. C. BUCKNILL, M.D. F.R.S. Second Edition. Crown 8vo. 6s. 6d.

BULLOCK.—*Works by* W. H. BULLOCK.

Polish Experiences during the Insurrection of 1863-4.
Crown 8vo. With Map. 8*s.* 6*d.*

Across Mexico in 1864-5.
With Coloured Map and Illustrations. Crown 8vo. 10*s.* 6*d.*

BURGON.—*A Treatise on the Pastoral Office.*
Addressed chiefly to Candidates for Holy Orders, or to those who
have recently undertaken the cure of souls. By the Rev. JOHN
W. BURGON, M.A. 8vo. 12*s.*

BUTLER (ARCHER).—*Works by the Rev.* WILLIAM ARCHER
BUTLER, M.A. *late Professor of Moral Philosophy in the
University of Dublin.*

Sermons, Doctrinal and Practical.
Edited, with a Memoir of the Author's Life, by THOMAS WOOD-
WARD, M.A. Dean of Down. With Portrait. *Seventh and
Cheaper Edition.* 8vo. 8*s.*

A Second Series of Sermons.
Edited by J. A. JEREMIE, D.D. Regius Professor of Divinity at
Cambridge. *Fifth and Cheaper Edition.* 8vo. 7*s.*

History of Ancient Philosophy.
Edited by WM. H. THOMPSON, M.A. Master of Trinity College,
Cambridge. Two Vols. 8vo. 1*l.* 5*s.*

*Letters on Romanism, in reply to Dr. Newman's Essay
on Development.*
Edited by the Dean of Down. *Second Edition,* revised by
Archdeacon HARDWICK. 8vo. 10*s.* 6*d.*

BUTLER (MONTAGU).—*Sermons preached in the Chapel of
Harrow School.*
By H. MONTAGU BUTLER, Head Master. Crown 8vo. 7*s.* 6*d.*

BUTLER (GEORGE).—*Works by the Rev.* GEORGE BUTLER.

Family Prayers.
Crown 8vo. 5*s.*

Sermons preached in Cheltenham College Chapel.
Crown 8vo. 7*s.* 6*d.*

CAIRNES.—*The Slave Power; its Character, Career, and
Probable Designs.*
Being an Attempt to Explain the Real Issues Involved in the
American Contest. By J. E. CAIRNES, M.A. *Second Edition.*
8vo. 10*s.* 6*d.*

CALDERWOOD.—*Philosophy of the Infinite.*
A Treatise on Man's Knowledge of the Infinite Being, in answer to Sir W. Hamilton and Dr. Mansel. By the Rev. HENRY CALDERWOOD, M.A. Professor of Moral Philosophy at Edinburgh. *Second Edition.* 8vo. 14s.

Cambridge   Senate-House   Problems   and   Riders,   with Solutions.

1848—1851.—*Problems.*
By FERRERS and JACKSON. 15s. 6d.

1848—1851.—*Riders.*
By JAMESON. 7s. 6d.

1854.—*Problems and Riders.*
By WALTON and MACKENZIE, M.A. 10s. 6d.

1857.—*Problems and Riders.*
. By CAMPION and WALTON. 8s. 6d.

1860.—*Problems and Riders.*
By WATSON and ROUTH. 7s. 6d.

1864.—*Problems and Riders.*
By WALTON and WILKINSON. 10s. 6d.

Cambridge Lent Sermons.—
Sermons preached during Lent, 1864, in Great St. Mary's Church, Cambridge. By the BISHOP of OXFORD, Rev. H. P. LIDDON, T. L. CLAUGHTON, J. R. WOODFORD, Dr. GOULBURN, J. W. BURGON, T. T. CARTER, Dr. PUSEY, DEAN HOOK, W. J. BUTLER, DEAN GOODWIN. Crown 8vo. 7s. 6d.

Cambridge Course of Elementary Natural Philosophy, for the Degree of B.A.
Originally compiled by J. C. SNOWBALL, M.A., late Fellow of St. John's College. *Fifth Edition,* revised and enlarged, and adapted for the Middle-Class Examinations by THOMAS LUND, B.D. Crown 8vo. 5s.

Cambridge and Dublin Mathematical Journal.
The Complete Work, in Nine Vols. 8vo. Cloth. 7l. 4s. Only a few copies remain on hand.

Cambridge Characteristics in the Seventeenth Century.
By JAMES BASS MULLINGER, B.A. Crown 8vo. 4s. 6d.

CAMPBELL.—*Works by* JOHN M'LEOD CAMPBELL.

Thoughts on Revelation, with Special Reference to the Present Time.
Crown 8vo. 5s.

The Nature of the Atonement, and its Relation to Remission of Sins and Eternal Life.
Third Edition. With an Introduction and Notes. 8vo. 10s. 6d.

CARTER.—*King's College Chapel : Notes on its History and present condition.*
By T. J. P. CARTER, M.A. Fellow of King's College, Cambridge. With Photographs. 8vo. 5s.

Catullus.
Edited by R. ELLIS. 18mo. 3s. 6d.

CHALLIS.—*Creation in Plan and in Progress :*
Being an Essay on the First Chapter of Genesis. By the Rev. JAMES CHALLIS, M.A. F.R.S. F.R.A.S. Crown 8vo. 3s. 6d.

CHATTERTON.—*Leonore; a Tale.*
By GEORGIANA LADY CHATTERTON. *A New Edition.* Beautifully printed on thick toned paper. Crown 8vo. with Frontispiece and Vignette Title engraved by JEENS. 7s. 6d.

CHEYNE.—*Works by* C. H. H. CHEYNE, B.A.

An Elementary Treatise on the Planetary Theory.
With a Collection of Problems. Crown 8vo. 6s. 6d.

The Earth's Motion of Rotation (including the Theory of Precession and Nutation).
Crown 8vo. 3s. 6d.

Choice Notes on St. Matthew, drawn from Old and New Sources.
Crown 8vo. 4s. 6d.

CHRISTIE (J. R.).—*Elementary Test Questions in Pure and Mixed Mathematics.*
Crown 8vo. 8s. 6d.

Church Congress (Authorized Report of) held at Wolverhampton in October, 1867.
8vo. 3s. 6d.

CHURCH.—*Sermons preached before the University of Oxford.*
By R. W. CHURCH, M.A. late Fellow of Oriel College, Rector of Whatley. Extra fcap. 8vo. 4s. 6d.

CICERO.—*The Second Philippic Oration.*
With an Introduction and Notes, translated from KARL HALM. Edited, with Corrections and Additions, by JOHN E. B. MAYOR, M.A. *Third Edition.* Fcap. 8vo. 5s.

CLARK.—*Four Sermons preached in the Chapel of Trinity College, Cambridge.*
By W. G. CLARK, M.A. Fcap. 8vo. 2s. 6d.

CLAY.—*The Prison Chaplain.*
A Memoir of the Rev. JOHN CLAY, B.D. late Chaplain of the Preston Goal. With Selections from his Reports and Correspondence, and a Sketch of Prison Discipline in England. By his Son, the Rev. W. L. CLAY, M.A. 8vo. 15s.

The Power of the Keys.
Sermons preached in Coventry. By the Rev. W. L. CLAY, M.A. Fcap. 8vo. 3s. 6d.

Clergyman's Self-Examination concerning the Apostles' Creed.
Extra fcap. 8vo. 1s. 6d.

CLOUGH.—*The Poems of Arthur Hugh Clough,*
sometime Fellow of Oriel College, Oxford. With a Memoir by F. T. PALGRAVE. *Second Edition.* Fcap. 8vo. 6s.

COLENSO.—*Works by the Right Rev. J. W. COLENSO, D.D. Bishop of Natal.*

The Colony of Natal.
A Journal of Visitation. With a Map and Illustrations. Fcap. 8vo. 5s.

Village Sermons.
Second Edition. Fcap. 8vo. 2s. 6d.

Four Sermons on Ordination and on Missions.
18mo. 1s.

Companion to the Holy Communion,
Containing the Service and Select Readings from the writings of Professor MAURICE. *Fine Edition* morocco, antique style, 6s. *Common paper,* 1s.

Letter to His Grace the Archbishop of Canterbury,
Upon the Question of Polygamy, as found already existing in Converts from Heathenism. *Second Edition.* Crown 8vo. 1s. 6d.

Connells of Castle Connell.
By JANET GORDON. Two Vols. Crown 8vo. 21s.

COOPER.—*Athenae Cantabrigienses.*
By CHARLES HENRY COOPER, F.S.A. and THOMPSON COOPER, F.S.A. Vol. I. 8vo. 1500—85, 18s. Vol. II. 1586—1609, 18s.

COPE.—*An Introduction to Aristotle's Rhetoric.*
> With Analysis, Notes, and Appendices. By E. M. COPE,
> Senior Fellow and Tutor of Trinity College, Cambridge.
> 8vo. 14s.

COTTON.—*Works by the late* GEORGE EDWARD LYNCH
COTTON, D.D. *Bishop of Calcutta.*
*Sermons and Addresses delivered in Marlborough College
during Six Years.*
> Crown 8vo. 10s. 6d.

Sermons, chiefly connected with Public Events of 1854.
> Fcap. 8vo. 3s.

Sermons preached to English Congregations in India.
> Crown 8vo. 7s. 6d.

*Expository Sermons on the Epistles for the Sundays of
the Christian Year.*
> Two Vols. Crown 8vo. 15s.

COX.—*Recollections of Oxford.*
> By G. V. Cox, M.A. late Esquire Bedel and Coroner in the
> University of Oxford. Crown 8vo. 10s. 6d.

CRAIK.—*My First Journal.*
> A Book for the Young. By GEORGIANA M. CRAIK, Author of
> "Riverston," "Lost and Won," &c. Royal 16mo. Cloth, gilt
> leaves, 3s. 6d.

CURE.—*The Seven Words of Christ on the Cross.*
> Sermons preached at St. George's, Bloomsbury. By the Rev. E.
> CAPEL CURE, M.A. Fcap. 8vo. 3s. 6d.

DALTON.—*Arithmetical Examples progressively arranged;
together with Miscellaneous Exercises and Examination
Papers.*
> By the Rev. T. DALTON, M.A. Assistant Master at Eton
> College. 18mo. 2s 6d.

DANTE.—*Dante's Comedy, The Hell.*
> Translated by W. M. ROSSETTI. Fcap. 8vo. cloth. 5s.

DAVIES.—*Works by the Rev.* J. LLEWELYN DAVIES, M.A.
Rector of Christ Church, St. Marylebone, &c.
Sermons on the Manifestation of the Son of God.
> With a Preface addressed to Laymen on the present position of
> the Clergy of the Church of England; and an Appendix, on the
> Testimony of Scripture and the Church as to the Possibility
> of Pardon in the Future State. Fcap. 8vo. 6s. 6d.

DAVIES.—*The Work of Christ; or, the World Reconciled to God.*
With a Preface on the Atonement Controversy. Fcap. 8vo. 6s.

Baptism, Confirmation, and the Lord's Supper.
As interpreted by their outward signs. Three Expository Addresses for Parochial Use. Fcap. 8vo. Limp cloth. 1s. 6d.

Morality according to the Sacrament of the Lord's Supper.
Crown 8vo. 3s. 6d.

The Epistles of St. Paul to the Ephesians, the Colossians, and Philemon.
With Introductions and Notes, and an Essay on the Traces of Foreign Elements in the Theology of these Epistles. 8vo. 7s. 6d.

DAWSON.—*Acadian Geology, the Geological Structure, Organic Remains, and Mineral Resources of Nova Scotia, New Brunswick, and Prince Edward Island.*
By J. W. DAWSON, LL.D. F.R.S. F.G.S. *Second Edition,* revised and enlarged, with Geological Maps and Illustrations. 8vo. 18s.

DAY.—*Properties of Conic Sections proved Geometrically.*
By the Rev. H. G. DAY, M.A. Head-Master of Sedburgh Grammar School. Crown 8vo. 3s. 6d.

Days of Old; Stories from Old English History.
By the Author of "Ruth and her Friends." *New Edition,* 18mo. cloth, gilt leaves. 3s. 6d.

Demosthenes, De Corona.
The Greek Text with English Notes. By B. DRAKE, M.A. *Third Edition,* to which is prefixed ÆSCHINES AGAINST CTESIPHON, with English Notes. Fcap 8vo. 5s.

DE TEISSIER.—*Works by* G. F. DE TEISSIER, B.D.

Village Sermons.
Crown 8vo. 9s.

Second Series.
Crown 8vo. 8s. 6d.

The House of Prayer; or, a Practical Exposition of the Order for Morning and Evening Prayer in the Church of England.
18mo. extra cloth. 4s. 6d.

DE VERE.—*The Infant Bridal, and other Poems.*
By AUBREY DE VERE. Fcap. 8vo. 7s. 6d.

DILKE.—*Greater Britain.*
A Record of Travel in English-speaking Countries during 1866–7. (America, Australia, India.) By CHARLES WENTWORTH DILKE. Two Vols. 8vo. 28*s.*

DODGSON.—*Elementary Treatise on Determinants.*
By C. L. DODGSON, M.A. 4to. 10*s.* 6*d.*

DONALDSON.—*A Critical History of Christian Literature and Doctrine, from the Death of the Apostles to the Nicene Council.*
By JAMES DONALDSON, LL.D. Three Vols. 8vo. cloth. 31*s.*

DOYLE.—*The Return of the Guards, and other Poems.*
By Sir FRANCIS HASTINGS DOYLE, Professor of Poetry in the University of Oxford. Fcap. 8vo. 7*s.*

DREW.—*Works by* W. H. DREW, M.A.

A Geometrical Treatise on Conic Sections.
Third Edition. Crown 8vo. 4*s.* 6*d.*

Solutions to Problems contained in Drew's Treatise on Conic Sections.
Crown 8vo. 4*s.* 6*d.*

Early Egyptian History for the Young.
With Descriptions of the Tombs and Monuments. *New Edition,* with Frontispiece. Fcap. 8vo. 5*s.*

EASTWOOD.—*The Bible Word Book.*
A Glossary of Old English Bible Words. By J. EASTWOOD, M.A. of St. John's College, and W. ALDIS WRIGHT, M.A. Trinity College, Cambridge. 18mo. 5*s.* 6*d.* Uniform with Macmillan's School Class Books.

Ecce Homo.
A Survey of the Life and Work of Jesus Christ. 23d Thousand. Crown 8vo. 6*s.*

Echoes of Many Voices from Many Lands.
By A. F. 18mo. cloth, extra gilt. 3*s.* 6*d.*

ELLICE.—*English Idylls.*
By JANE ELLICE. Fcap. 8vo. cloth. 6*s.*

ELLIOTT.—*Life of Henry Venn Elliott, of Brighton.*
By JOSIAH BATEMAN, M.A. Author of "Life of Daniel Wilson, Bishop of Calcutta," &c. With Portrait, engraved by JEENS. Crown 8vo. 8*s.* 6*d.*

Essays on Church Policy.
Edited by the Rev. W. L. CLAY, M.A. Incumbent of Rainhill, Lancashire. 8vo. 9s.

Essays on a Liberal Education.
By Various Writers. Edited by the Rev. F. W. FARRAR, M.A. F.R.S. &c. *Second Edition.* 8vo. 10s. 6d.

EVANS.—*Brother Fabian's Manuscript, and other Poems.*
By SEBASTIAN EVANS. Fcap. 8vo. cloth. 6s.

FARRAR.—*The Fall of Man, and other Sermons.*
By the Rev. F. W. FARRAR, M.A. late Fellow of Trinity College, Cambridge. Fcap, 8vo. 6s.

FAWCETT.— *Works by* HENRY FAWCETT, *M.P.*
The Economic Position of the British Labourer.
Extra fcap. 8vo. 5s.

Manual of Political Economy.
Second Edition. Crown 8vo. 12s.

Fellowship: Letters addressed to my Sister Mourners.
Fcap. 8vo. cloth gilt. 3s. 6d.

FERRERS.—*A Treatise on Trilinear Co-ordinates, the Method of Reciprocal Polars, and the Theory of Projections.*
By the Rev. N. M. FERRERS, M.A. *Second Edition.* Crown 8vo. 6s. 6d.

FLETCHER.—*Thoughts from a Girl's Life.*
By LUCY FLETCHER. *Second Edition.* Fcap. 8vo. 4s. 6d.

FORBES.—*Life of Edward Forbes, F.R.S.*
By GEORGE WILSON, M.D. F.R.S.E., and ARCHIBALD GEIKIE, F.R.S. 8vo. with Portrait. 14s.

FORBES.—*The Voice of God in the Psalms.*
By GRANVILLE FORBES, Rector of Broughton. Crown 8vo. 6s. 6d.

FOX.—*On the Diagnosis and Treatment of the Varieties of Dyspepsia, considered in Relation to the Pathological Origin of the different Forms of Indigestion.*
By WILSON FOX, M.D. Lond. F.R.C.P. Holme Professor of Clinical Medicine at University College, London, and Physician to University College Hospital. *Second Edition.* Demy 8vo. 7s. 6d.

On the Artificial Production of Tubercle in the Lower Animals.
4to. 5s. 6d.

FREELAND.—*The Fountain of Youth.*
Translated from the Danish of Frederick Paludan Müller. By
HUMPHREY WILLIAM FREELAND, late M.P. for Chichester.
With Illustrations designed by Walter Allen. Crown 8vo. 6s.

FREEMAN.—*History of Federal Government from the Foundation of the Achaian League to the Disruption of the United States.*
By EDWARD A. FREEMAN, M.A. Vol. I. General Introduction.
—History of the Greek Federations. 8vo. 21s.

FRENCH.—*Notes on the Characters in Shakespeare's Plays.*
By G. R. FRENCH. [In the Press.

FROST.—*The First Three Sections of Newton's Principia.*
With Notes and Problems in Illustration of the Subject. By
PERCIVAL FROST, M.A. *Second Edition.* 8vo. 10s. 6d.

FROST AND WOLSTENHOLME.—*A Treatise on Solid Geometry.*
By the Rev. PERCIVAL FROST, M.A. and the Rev. J. WOLSTENHOLME, M.A. 8vo. 18s.

The Sicilian Expedition.
Being Books VI. and VII. of Thucydides, with Notes. By the
Rev. P. FROST, M.A. Fcap. 8vo. 5s.

FURNIVALL.—*Le Morte Arthur.*
Edited from the Harleian M.S. 2252, in the British Museum.
By F. J. FURNIVALL, M.A. With Essay by the late HERBERT
COLERIDGE. Fcap. 8vo. 7s. 6d.

GALTON.—*Meteorographica, or Methods of Mapping the Weather.*
Illustrated by upwards of 600 Printed Lithographed Diagrams.
By FRANCIS GALTON, F.R.S. 4to. 9s.

GEIKIE.—*Works by* ARCHIBALD GEIKIE, F.R.S. *Director of the Geological Survey of Scotland.*

Story of a Boulder; or, Gleanings by a Field Geologist.
Illustrated with Woodcuts. Crown 8vo. 5s.

Scenery of Scotland, viewed in connexion with its Physical Geology.
With Illustrations and a New Geological Map. Crown 8vo.
10s. 6d.

Elementary Lessons in Physical Geology. [In the Press.

GIFFORD.—*The Glory of God in Man.*
By E. H. GIFFORD, D.D. Fcap. 8vo. 3s. 6d.

Globe Editions :

The Complete Works of William Shakespeare.
Edited by W. G. CLARK and W. ALDIS WRIGHT. Ninety-first Thousand. Globe 8vo. 3*s.* 6*d.* ; paper covers, 2*s.* 6*d.*

Morte DArthur.
SIR THOMAS MALORY'S Book of KING ARTHUR and of his noble KNIGHTS of the ROUND TABLE. The Edition of Caxton, revised for Modern use. With an Introduction by SIR EDWARD STRACHEY, Bart. Globe 8vo. 3*s.* 6*d.*

The Poetical Works of Sir Walter Scott.
With Biographical Essay by F. T. PALGRAVE.

The Poetical Works and Letters of Robert Burns.
Edited, with Life, by ALEXANDER SMITH. Globe 8vo. 3*s.* 6*d.*

The Adventures of Robinson Crusoe.
Edited, with Introduction, by HENRY KINGSLEY. Globe 8vo. 3*s.* 6*d.*

Goldsmith's Miscellaneous Works.
With Biographical Essay by PROF. MASSON. Globe 8vo. 3*s.* 6*d.*
Other Standard Works are in the Press.

Globe Atlas of Europe.
Uniform in Size with MACMILLAN'S GLOBE SERIES. Containing Forty-Eight Coloured Maps on the same scale, Plans of London and Paris, and a Copious Index. Strongly bound in half morocco, with flexible back, 9*s.*

GODFRAY.—An Elementary Treatise on the Lunar Theory.
With a brief Sketch of the Problem up to the time of Newton. By HUGH GODFRAY, M.A. *Second Edition revised.* Crown 8vo. 5*s.* 6*d.*

A Treatise on Astronomy, for the Use of Colleges and Schools.
By HUGH GODFRAY, M.A. 8vo. 12*s.* 6*d.*

Golden Treasury Series :
Uniformly printed in 18mo. with Vignette Titles by Sir NOEL PATON, T. WOOLNER, W. HOLMAN HUNT, J. E. MILLAIS, ARTHUR HUGHES, &c. Engraved on Steel by JEENS. Bound in extra cloth, 4*s.* 6*d.* ; morocco plain, 7*s.* 6*d.* ; morocco extra, 10*s.* 6*d.* each volume.

The Golden Treasury of the Best Songs and Lyrical Poems in the English Language.
Selected and arranged, with Notes, by FRANCIS TURNER PALGRAVE.

The Children's Garland from the Best Poets.
Selected and arranged by COVENTRY PATMORE.

Golden **Treasury Series**—*continued.*

The Book of Praise.
From the Best English Hymn Writers. Selected and arranged by Sir ROUNDELL PALMER. *A New and Enlarged Edition.*

The Fairy Book : the Best Popular Fairy Stories.
Selected and rendered anew by the Author of "John Halifax, Gentleman."

The Ballad Book.
A Selection of the choicest British Ballads. Edited by WILLIAM ALLINGHAM.

The Jest Book.
The choicest Anecdotes and Sayings. Selected and arranged by MARK LEMON.

Bacon's Essays and Colours of Good and Evil.
With Notes and Glossarial Index, by W. ALDIS WRIGHT, M.A.
* Large paper copies, crown 8vo. 7*s.* 6*d.* ; or bound in half morocco, 10*s.* 6*d.*

The Pilgrim's Progress
From this World to that which is to Come. By JOHN BUNYAN.
* Large paper copies, crown 8vo. cloth, 7*s.* 6*d.*; or bound in half morocco, 10*s.* 6*d.*

The Sunday Book of Poetry for the Young.
Selected and arranged by C. F. ALEXANDER.

A Book of Golden Deeds of all Times and all Countries.
Gathered and Narrated anew by the Author of "The Heir of Redclyffe."

The Poetical Works of Robert Burns.
Edited, with Biographical Memoir, by ALEXANDER SMITH. Two Vols.

The Adventures of Robinson Crusoe.
Edited from the Original Editions by J. W. CLARK, M.A.

The Republic of Plato.
Translated into English with Notes by J. LL. DAVIES, M.A. and D. J. VAUGHAN, M.A.

The Song Book.
Words and Tunes from the best Poets and Musicians, selected and arranged by JOHN HULLAH.

La Lyre Française.
Selected and arranged, with Notes, by GUSTAVE MASSON.

Tom Brown's School Days.
By an OLD BOY.

GREEN.—*Spiritual Philosophy.*
Founded on the Teaching of the late SAMUEL TAYLOR COLE-
RIDGE. By the late JOSEPH HENRY GREEN, F.R.S. D.C.L.
Edited, with a Memoir of the Author's Life, by JOHN SIMON,
F.R.S. Two Vols. 8vo. cloth. **25s.**

Guesses at Truth.
By Two BROTHERS. With Vignette Title and Frontispiece.
New Edition. Fcap. 8vo. **6s.**

GUIZOT, M.—*Memoir of M. de Barante.*
Translated by the Author of "John Halifax, Gentleman."
Crown 8vo. **6s. 6d.**

Guide to the Unprotected
In Every Day Matters relating to Property and Income. By a
BANKER'S DAUGHTER. *Third Edition.* Extra fcap. 8vo.
3s. 6d.

HAMERTON.—*A Painter's Camp in the Highlands.*
By P. G. HAMERTON. *New and Cheaper Edition,* one vol.
Extra fcap. 8vo. **6s.**

Etching and Etchers.
A Treatise Critical and Practical. By P. G. HAMERTON. With
Original Plates by REMBRANDT, CALLOT, DUJARDIN, PAUL
POTTER, &c. Royal 8vo. Half morocco. **31s. 6d.**

HAMILTON.—*On Truth and Error.*
Thoughts on the Principles of Truth, and the Causes and Effect
of Error. By JOHN HAMILTON. Crown 8vo. **5s.**

HARDWICK.—*Works by the Ven.* ARCHDEACON HARDWICK.
Christ and other Masters.
A Historical Inquiry into some of the Chief Parallelisms and
Contrasts between Christianity and the Religious Systems of the
Ancient World. *New Edition,* revised, and a Prefatory Memoir
by the Rev. FRANCIS PROCTER. Two vols. crown 8vo. **15s.**

A History of the Christian Church.
Middle Age. From Gregory the Great to the Excommunication
of Luther. Edited by FRANCIS PROCTER, M.A. With Four
Maps constructed for this work by A. KEITH JOHNSTON. *Second
Edition.* Crown 8vo. **10s. 6d.**

*A History of the Christian Church during the Refor-
mation.*
Revised by FRANCIS PROCTER, M.A. *Second Edition.* Crown
8vo. **10s. 6d.**

Twenty Sermons for Town Congregations.
Crown 8vo. **6s. 6d.**

HELPS.—*Realmah.*
By ARTHUR HELPS. Two vols. crown 8vo. **16s.**

HEMMING.—*An Elementary Treatise on the Differential and Integral Calculus.*
By G. W. HEMMING, M.A. *Second Edition.* 8vo. *9s.*

HERSCHEL.—*The Iliad of Homer.*
Translated into English Hexameters. By Sir JOHN HERSCHEL, Bart. 8vo. *18s.*

HERVEY.—*The Genealogies of our Lord and Saviour Jesus Christ,*
As contained in the Gospels of St. Matthew and St. Luke, reconciled with each other, and shown to be in harmony with the true Chronology of the Times. By Lord ARTHUR HERVEY, M.A. 8vo. *10s. 6d.*

HERVEY (ROSAMOND). *Works by* ROSAMOND HERVEY.

The Aarbergs.
Two vols. crown 8vo. cloth. *21s.*

Duke Ernest,
A Tragedy ; and other Poems. Fcap. 8vo. *6s.*

HILL (FLORENCE).—*Children of the State. The Training of Juvenile Paupers.*
Extra fcap. cloth. *5s.*

Historical Selections.
A Series of Readings from the best Authorities on English and European History. Selected and Arranged by E. M. SEWELL and C. M. YONGE. Extra fcap. 8vo. *6s.*

HISTORICUS.—*Letters on some Questions of International Law.*
Reprinted from the *Times*, with considerable Additions. 8vo. *7s. 6d.* Also, ADDITIONAL LETTERS. 8vo. *2s. 6d.*

HODGSON.—*Mythology for Latin Versification.*
A Brief Sketch of the Fables of the Ancients, prepared to be rendered into Latin Verse for Schools. By F. HODGSON, B.D. late Provost of Eton. *New Edition*, revised by F. C. HODGSON, M.A. 18mo. *3s.*

HOLE.—*Works by* CHARLES HOLE, M.A. *Trinity College, Cambridge.*

A Brief Biographical Dictionary.
Compiled and arranged by CHARLES HOLE, M.A. Trinity College, Cambridge. In pott 8vo. neatly and strongly bound in cloth. *Second Edition.* *4s. 6d.*

Genealogical Stemma of the Kings of England and France.
In One Sheet. *1s.*

B

HORNER.—*The Tuscan Poet Guiseppe Giusti and his Times.*
By SUSAN HORNER. Crown 8vo. 7s. 6d.

HOWARD.—*The Pentateuch ;*
Or, the Five Books of Moses. Translated into English from the
Version of the LXX. With Notes on its Omissions and Inser-
tions, and also on the Passages in which it differs from the
Authorized Version. By the Hon. HENRY HOWARD, D.D.
Crown 8vo. GENESIS, One Volume, 8s. 6d. ; EXODUS AND
LEVITICUS, One Volume, 10s. 6d.; NUMBERS AND DEUTER-
ONOMY, One Volume, 10s. 6d.

HOZIER.—*The Seven Weeks' War ;*
Its Antecedents and its Incidents. By H. M. HOZIER. With
Maps and Plans. Two Vols. 8vo. 28s.

HUMPHRY.—*The Human Skeleton (including the Joints).*
By G. M. HUMPHRY, M.D., F.R.S. With Two Hundred and
Sixty Illustrations drawn from Nature. Medium 8vo. 1l. 8s.

HUXLEY.—*Lessons in Elementary Physiology.*
With numerous Illustrations. By T. H. HUXLEY, F.R.S.
Professor of Natural History in the Royal School of Mines.
Uniform with Macmillans' School Class Books. *Second Edition.*
18mo. 4s. 6d.

Hymni Ecclesiæ.
Fcap. 8vo. 7s. 6d.

IRVING.—*Annals of our Own Time.*
A Diurnal of Events, Social and Political, which have happened
in or had relation to the Kingdom of Great Britain from the
Accession of Queen Victoria to the present Year. By JOSEPH
IRVING. 8vo. [In the Press.

JAMESON.—*Works by the Rev. F. J. JAMESON, M.A.*

Life's Work, in Preparation and in Retrospect.
Sermons preached before the University of Cambridge. Fcap.
8vo. 1s. 6d.

Brotherly Counsels to Students.
Sermons preached in the Chapel of St. Catharine's College,
Cambridge. Fcap. 8vo. 1s. 6d.

JEVONS.—*The Coal Question.*
By W. STANLEY JEVONS, M.A. Fellow of University College,
London. *Second Edition, revised.* 8vo. 10s. 6d.

JONES.—*The Church of England and Common Sense.*
By HARRY JONES, M.A. Fcap. 8vo. 3s. 6d.

JONES.—*Algebraical Exercises,*
Progressively Arranged by the Rev. C. A. JONES, M.A. and
C. H. CHEYNE, M.A. Mathematical Masters in Westminster
School. 18mo. 2s. 6d.

Journal of Anatomy and Physiology.
> Conducted by Professors HUMPHRY and NEWTON, and Mr.
> CLARK of Cambridge ; Professor TURNER, of Edinburgh ; and
> Dr. WRIGHT, of Dublin. Published twice a year. Price to
> subscribers, 14s. per annum. Price 7s. 6d. each Part. Vol. 1.
> containing Parts I. and II. Royal 8vo. 16s. Part III. 6s.

JUVENAL, *for Schools.*
> With English Notes. By J. E. B. MAYOR, M.A. *New and
> Cheaper Edition.* Crown 8vo. [In the Press.

KEARY.—*The Little Wanderlin,*
> And other Fairy Tales. By A. and E. KEARY. 18mo. 3s. 6d.

KEMPIS (THOS. A).—*De Imitatione Christi. Libri IV.*
> Borders in the ancient style, after Holbein, Durer, and other
> old Masters, containing Dances of Death, Acts of Mercy,
> Emblems, and a variety of curious ornamentation. In white
> cloth, extra gilt. 7s. 6d.

KENNEDY.—*Legendary Fictions of the Irish Celts.*
> Collected and Narrated by PATRICK KENNEDY. Crown 8vo.
> 7s. 6d.

KINGSBURY.—*Spiritual Sacrifice and Holy Communion.*
> Seven Sermons preached during the Lent of 1867 at St. Leo-
> nard's-on-Sea, with Notes. By T. L. KINGSBURY, M.A. late
> Rector of Chetwynd. Fcap. 8vo. 3s. 6d.

KINGSLEY.—*Works by the Rev.* CHARLES KINGSLEY, M.A.
*Rector of Eversley, and Professor of Modern History in
the University of Cambridge.*

The Roman and the Teuton.
> A Series of Lectures delivered before the University of Cam-
> bridge. 8vo. 12s.

Two Years Ago.
> *Fourth Edition.* Crown 8vo. 6s.

" Westward Ho ! "
> *Fifth Edition.* Crown 8vo. 6s.

Alton Locke.
> *New Edition.* With a New Preface. Crown 8vo. 4s. 6d.

Hypatia.
> *Fourth Edition.* Crown 8vo. 6s.

Yeast.
> *Fifth Edition.* Crown 8vo. 5s.

Hereward the Wake—Last of the English.
> Crown 8vo. 6s.

KINGSLEY (*Rev.* CHARLES).—*The Saint's Tragedy.*
   Third Edition. Fcap. 8vo. 5s.

Andromeda,
   And other Poems. *Third Edition.* Fcap. 8vo. 5s.

The Water Babies.
   A Fairy Tale for a Land Baby. With Two Illustrations by Sir
   NOEL PATON, R.S.A. *Third Edition.* Crown 8vo. 6s.

The Heroes;
   Or, Greek Fairy Tales for my Children. With Coloured Illustrations. *New Edition.* 18mo. 4s. 6d.

*Three Lectures delivered at the Royal Institution on the
   Ancien Regime.*
   Crown 8vo. 6s.

The Water of Life,
   And other Sermons. Fcap. 8vo. 6s.

Village Sermons.
   Seventh Edition. Fcap. 8vo. 2s. 6d.

The Gospel of the Pentateuch.
   Second Edition. Fcap. 8vo. 4s. 6d.

Good News of God.
   Fourth Edition. Fcap. 8vo. 4s. 6d.

Sermons for the Times.
   Third Edition. Fcap. 8vo. 3s. 6d.

Town and Country Sermons.
   Extra fcap. 8vo. *New Edition.* 6s.

Sermons on National Subjects.
   First Series. *Second Edition.* Fcap. 8vo. 5s.
   Second Series. *Second Edition.* Fcap. 8vo. 5s.

Discipline,
   And other Sermons. Fcap. 8vo. 6s.

Alexandria and her Schools.
   With a Preface. Crown 8vo. 5s.

The Limits of Exact Science as applied to History.
   An Inaugural Lecture delivered before the University of Cambridge. Crown 8vo. 2s.

Phaethon; or, Loose Thoughts for Loose Thinkers.
   Third Edition. Crown 8vo. 2s.

David.
   Four Sermons : David's Weakness—David's Strength—David's
   Anger—David's Deserts. Fcap. 8vo. cloth. 2s. 6d.

KINGSLEY.— *Works by* HENRY KINGSLEY.

Austin Elliot.
New Edition. Crown 8vo. 6s.

The Recollections of Geoffry Hamlyn.
Second Edition. Crown 8vo. 6s.

The Hillyars and the Burtons: A Story of Two Families.
Crown 8vo. 6s.

Ravenshoe.
New Edition. Crown 8vo. 6s.

Leighton Court.
New Edition. Crown 8vo. 6s.

Silcote of Silcotes.
Three Vols. Crown 8vo. 31s. 6d.

KIRCHHOFF.—*Researches on the Solar Spectrum and the Spectra of the Chemical Elements.*
By G. KIRCHHOFF, of Heidelberg. Translated by HENRY E. ROSCOE, B.A. Second Part. 4to. 5s. with 2 Plates.

KITCHENER.—*Geometrical Note Book,*
Containing Easy Problems in Geometrical Drawing, preparatory to the Study of Geometry. For the Use of Schools. By F. E. KITCHENER, M.A., Mathematical Master at Rugby. 4to. 2s.

LANCASTER.— *Works by* WILLIAM LANCASTER.

Præterita.
Poems. Extra fcap. 8vo. 4s. 6d.

Studies in Verse.
Extra fcap. 8vo. 4s. 6d.

Eclogues and Mono-dramas ; or, a Collection of Verses.
Extra fcap. 8vo. 4s. 6d.

LATHAM.—*The Construction of Wrought-iron Bridges.*
Embracing the Practical Application of the Principles of Mechanics to Wrought-Iron Girder Work. By J. H. LATHAM, Civil Engineer. 8vo. With numerous detail Plates. *Second Edition.* [Preparing.

LATHAM.—*Black and White: A Three Months' Tour in the United States.*
By H. LATHAM, M.A. Barrister-at-Law. 8vo. 10s. 6d.

LAW.—*The Alps of Hannibal.*
By WILLIAM JOHN LAW, M.A. Two vols. 8vo. 21s.

Lectures to Ladies on Practical Subjects.
>*Third Edition, revised.* Crown 8vo. 7s. 6d.

LEMON.—*Legends of Number Nip.*
>By MARK LEMON. With Six Illustrations by CHARLES KEENE. Extra fcap. 8vo. 5s.

LIGHTFOOT.— *Works by J. B. LIGHTFOOT, D.D. Hulsean Professor of Divinity in the University of Cambridge.*
>*St. Paul's Epistle to the Galatians.*
>>A Revised Text, with Notes and Dissertations. *Second Edition, revised.* 8vo. 12s.

>*St. Paul's Epistle to the Philippians.*
>>A Revised Text, with Notes and Dissertations. 8vo. 12s.

Little Estella.
>And other Fairy Tales for the Young. Royal 16mo. 3s. 6d.

LIVERPOOL.—*The Life and Administration of Robert Banks, Second Earl of Liverpool.*
>Compiled from Original Documents by PROFESSOR YONGE. 3 vols. 8vo. 42s.

LOCKYER. — *Elementary Lessons in Astronomy. With numerous Illustrations.*
>By J. NORMAN LOCKYER, F.R.A.S. 18mo. 5s. 6d.

LUCKOCK.—*The Tables of Stone.*
>A Course of Sermons preached in All Saints', Cambridge, by H. M. LUCKOCK, M.A., Vicar. Fcap. 8vo. 3s. 6d.

LUDLOW and HUGHES.—*A Sketch of the History of the United States from Independence to Secession.*
>By J. M. LUDLOW, Author of "British India, its Races and its History," "The Policy of the Crown towards India," &c. To which is added, "The Struggle for Kansas." By THOMAS HUGHES, Author of "Tom Brown's School Days," "Tom Brown at Oxford," &c. Crown 8vo. 8s. 6d.

LUSHINGTON.—*The Italian War, 1848-9, and the Last Italian Poet.*
>By the late HENRY LUSHINGTON. With a Biographical Preface by G. S. VENABLES. Crown 8vo. 6s. 6d.

LYTTELTON.—*Works by LORD LYTTELTON.*
>*The Comus of Milton rendered into Greek Verse.*
>>Extra fcap. 8vo. *Second Edition.* 5s.

>*The Samson Agonistes of Milton rendered into Greek Verse.*
>>Extra fcap. 8vo. 6s. 6d.

MACKENZIE.—*The Christian Clergy of the First Ten Centuries, and their Influence on European Civilization.*
By HENRY MACKENZIE, B.A. Scholar of Trinity College, Cambridge. Crown 8vo. 6s. 6d.

MACLAREN.—*Sermons preached at Manchester.*
By ALEXANDER MACLAREN. Second Edition. Fcap. 8vo. 4s. 6d. A Second Series in the Press.

MACLAREN.—*Training, in Theory and Practice.*
By ARCHIBALD MACLAREN, Oxford. With Frontispiece, and other Illustrations. 8vo. Handsomely bound in cloth. 7s. 6d.

MACLEAR.—*Works by* G. F. MACLEAR, B.D. *Head Master of King's College School, and Preacher at the Temple Church :—*

A History of Christian Missions during the Middle Ages.
Crown 8vo. 10s. 6d.

The Witness of the Eucharist; or, The Institution and Early Celebration of the Lord's Supper, considered as an Evidence of the Historical Truth of the Gospel Narrative and of the Atonement.
Crown 8vo. 4s. 6d.

A Class-Book of Old Testament History.
With Four Maps. *Fourth Edition.* 18mo. 4s. 6d.

A Class-Book of New Testament History.
Including the connexion of the Old and New Testament. *Second Edition.* 18mo. 5s. 6d.

A Class-Book of the Catechism of the Church of England.
Second Edition. 18mo. cloth. 2s. 6d.

A Shilling Book of Old Testament History.
18mo. cloth limp. 1s.

A Shilling Book of New Testament History.
18mo. cloth limp. 1s.

A First Class-Book of the Catechism of the Church of England, with Scripture Proofs for Junior Classes and Schools.
6d.

MACMILLAN.—*Works by the Rev.* HUGH MACMILLAN.

Bible Teachings in Nature.
Second Edition. Crown 8vo. **6s.**

Foot-notes from the Page of Nature.
With numerous Illustrations. Fcap. 8vo. **5s.**

Macmillan's Magazine.
Published Monthly, price One Shilling. Volumes I.—XVIII. **are** now ready, **7s. 6d.** each.

MACMILLAN & CO.'S *Six Shilling Series of Works of Fiction.*

KINGSLEY.—*Works by the* REV. CHARLES KINGSLEY, M.A.
Westward Ho !
Hypatia.
Hereward the Wake—Last of the English.
Two Years Ago.

Works by the Author of " The Heir of Redclyffe."
The Heir of Redclyffe.
Dynevor Terrace ; or, The Clue of Life.
Heartsease ; or, The Brother's Wife.
The Clever Woman of the Family.
Hopes and Fears; or, Scenes from the Life of a Spinster
The Young Stepmother ; or, A Chronicle of Mistakes.
The Daisy Chain.
The Trial : More Links of the Daisy Chain.

KINGSLEY.—*Works by* HENRY KINGSLEY.
Geoffry Hamlyn.
Ravenshoe.
Austin Elliot.
Hillyars and Burtons.
Leighton Court.

TREVELYAN.—*Works by* G. O. TREVELYAN.

Cawnpore.

Competition Wallah.

MISCELLANEOUS.

The Moor Cottage.
By MAY BEVERLEY.

Janet's Home.

Tom Brown at Oxford.
By the Author of "Tom Brown's School Days.

Clemency Franklyn.
By the Author of "Janet's Home."

A Son of the Soil.

Old Sir Douglas.
By HON. MRS. NORTON.

McCOSH.—*Works by* JAMES McCOSH, LL.D. *Professor of Logic and Metaphysics, Queen's College, Belfast, &c.*

The Method of the Divine Government, Physical and Moral.
Ninth Edition. 8vo. 10s. 6d.

The Supernatural in Relation to the Natural.
Crown 8vo. 7s. 6d.

The Intuitions of the Mind.
A New Edition. 8vo. 10s. 6d.

An Examination of Mr. J. S. Mill's Philosophy.
Being a Defence of Fundamental Truth. Crown 8vo. 7s. 6d.

Philosophical Papers.
1. Examination of Sir W. Hamilton's Logic. II. Reply to Mr. Mill's. Third Edition. III. Present State of Moral Philosophy in Britain. 8vo. 3s. 6d.

MANSFIELD.—*Works by* C. B. MANSFIELD, M.A.

Paraguay, Brazil, and the Plate.
With a Map, and numerous Woodcuts. With a Sketch of his Life, by the Rev. CHARLES KINGSLEY. Crown 8vo. 12s. 6d.

A Theory of Salts.
A Treatise on the Constitution of Bipolar (two membered) Chemical Compounds. Crown 8vo. cloth. 14s.

MARKHAM.—*A History of the Abyssinian Expedition.*
 Including an Account of the Physical Geography, Geology, and Botany of the Region traversed by the English Forces. By CLEMENTS R. MARKHAM, F.R.G.S. With a Chapter by LIEUT. PRIDEAUX, containing a Narrative of his Mission and Captivity. With Maps, &c. 8vo.

MARRINER.—*Sermons preached at Lyme Regis.*
 By E. T. MARRINER, Curate. Fcap. 8vo. 4s. 6d.

MARSHALL.—*A Table of Irregular Greek Verbs.*
 8vo. 1s.

MARTIN.—*The Statesman's Year Book for* 1869. By FREDERICK MARTIN. *(Sixth Annual Publication.)*
 A Statistical, Mercantile, and Historical Account of the Civilized World for the Year 1868. Forming a Manual for Politicians and Merchants. Crown 8vo. 10s. 6d.

MARTINEAU.—*Biographical Sketches,* 1852–68.
 By HARRIET MARTINEAU.

MASSON.—*Works by* DAVID MASSON, M.A. *Professor of Rhetoric and English Literature in the University of Edinburgh.*

 Essays, Biographical and Critical.
  Chiefly on the English Poets. 8vo. 12s. 6d.

 British Novelists and their Styles.
  Being a Critical Sketch of the History of British Prose Fiction. Crown 8vo. 7s. 6d.

 Life of John Milton.
  Narrated in connexion with the Political, Ecclesiastical, and Literary History of his Time. Vol. I. with Portraits. 8vo. 18s.

 Recent British Philosophy.
  A Review, with Criticisms, including some Comments on Mr. Mill's Answer to Sir William Hamilton. *New and Cheaper Edition.* Crown 8vo. 6s.

MAUDSLEY.—*The Physiology and Pathology of the Mind.*
 By HENRY MAUDSLEY, M.D. *New and Revised Edition.* 8vo. 16s.

MAURICE.—*Works by the Rev.* FREDERICK DENISON MAURICE, M.A. *Professor of Moral Philosophy in the University of Cambridge.*

 The Conscience.
  Lectures on Casuistry, delivered in the University of Cambridge. 8vo. 8s. 6d.

MAURICE.—*The Claims of the Bible and of Science.*
A Correspondence on some Questions respecting the Pentateuch.
Crown 8vo. 4*s.* 6*d.*

Dialogues on Family Worship.
Crown 8vo. 6*s.*

The Patriarchs and Lawgivers of the Old Testament.
Third and Cheaper Edition. Crown 8vo. 5*s.*
This volume contains Discourses on the Pentateuch, Joshua,
Judges, and the beginning of the First Book of Samuel.

The Prophets and Kings of the Old Testament.
Second Edition. Crown 8vo. 10*s.* 6*d.*
This volume contains Discources on Samuel I. and II.; Kings I.
and II.; Amos, Joel, Hosea, Isaiah, Micah, Nahum, Habakkuk,
Jeremiah, and Ezekiel.

The Gospel of the Kingdom of Heaven.
A Series of Lectures on the Gospel of St. Luke. Crown 8vo. 9*s.*

The Gospel of St. John.
A Series of Discourses. *Third and Cheaper Edition.* Crown
8vo. 6*s.*

The Epistles of St. John.
A Series of Lectures on Christian Ethics. *Second and Cheaper
Edition.* Crown 8vo. 6*s.*

*The Commandments considered as Instruments of
National Reformation.*
Crown 8vo. 4*s.* 6*d.*

*Expository Sermons on the Prayer-book. The Prayer-
book considered especially in reference to the Romish
System.*
Second Edition. Fcap. 8vo. 5*s.* 6*d.*

Lectures on the Apocalypse,
Or Book of the Revelation of St. John the Divine. Crown 8vo.
10*s.* 6*d.*

What is Revelation?
A Series of Sermons on the Epiphany; to which are added
Letters to a Theological Student on the Bampton Lectures of
Mr. MANSEL. Crown 8vo. 10*s.* 6*d.*

Sequel to the Inquiry, " What is Revelation?".
Letters in Reply to Mr. Mansel's Examination of "Strictures on
the Bampton Lectures." Crown 8vo. 6*s.*

Lectures on Ecclesiastical History.
8vo. 10*s.* 6*d.*

MAURICE.—*Theological Essays.*
Second Edition. Crown 8vo. 10*s.* 6*d.*

The Doctrine of Sacrifice deduced from the Scriptures.
Crown 8vo. 7*s.* 6*d.*

The Religions of the World,
And their Relations to Christianity. *Fourth Edition.* Fcap.
8vo. 5*s.*

On the Lord's Prayer.
Fourth Edition. Fcap. 8vo. 2*s.* 6*d.*

On the Sabbath Day;
The Character of the Warrior; and on the Interpretation of
History. Fcap. 8vo. 2*s.* 6*d.*

Learning and Working.
Six Lectures on the Foundation of Colleges for Working Men.
Crown 8vo. 5*s.*

The Ground and Object of Hope for Mankind.
Four Sermons preached before the University of Cambridge.
Crown 8vo. 3*s.* 6*d.*

Law's Remarks on the Fable of the Bees.
With an Introduction by F. D. MAURICE, M.A. Fcap. 8vo.
4*s.* 6*d.*

MAYOR.—*A First Greek Reader.*
Edited after Karl Halm, with Corrections and Additions. By
JOHN E. B. MAYOR, M.A. Fcap. 8vo. 6*s.*

Autobiography of Matthew Robinson.
By JOHN E. B. MAYOR, M.A. Fcap. 8vo. 5*s.* 6*d.*

MERIVALE.—*Sallust for Schools.*
By C. MERIVALE, B.D. *Second Edition.* Fcap. 8vo. 4*s.* 6*d.*
₊ The Jugurtha and the Catalina may be had separately, price
2*s.* 6*d.* each.

Keats' Hyperion rendered into Latin Verse.
By C. MERIVALE, B.D. *Second Edition.* Extra fcap. 8vo.
3*s.* 6*d.*

MISTRAL, F.—*Mirelle, a Pastoral Epic of Provence.*
Translated by H. CRICHTON. Extra fcap. 8vo. 6*s.*

*Modern Industries: A Series of Reports on Industry and
Manufactures as represented in the Paris Exposition
in 1867.*
By TWELVE BRITISH WORKMEN. Crown 8vo. 1*s.*

MOORHOUSE.—*Works by* JAMES MOORHOUSE, M.A.
Some Modern Difficulties respecting the Facts of Nature and Revelation.
Fcap. 8vo. 2*s*. 6*d*.

The Hulsean Lectures for 1865.
Crown 8vo. 5*s*.

MORGAN.—*A Collection of Mathematical Problems and Examples.*
By H. A. MORGAN, M.A. Crown 8vo. 6*s*. 6*d*.

MORISON.—*The Life and Times of Saint Bernard, Abbot of Clairvaux.*
By JAMES COTTER MORISON, M.A. *New Edition, revised.* Crown 8vo. 7*s*. 6*d*.

MORLEY, JOHN.—*Edmund Burke—a Historical Study.*
Crown 8vo. 7*s*. 6*d*.

MORSE.—*Working for God,*
And other Practical Sermons. By FRANCIS MORSE, M.A. *Second Edition.* Fcap. 8vo. 5*s*.

MULLINGER.—*Cambridge Characteristics in the Seventeenth Century.*
By J. B. MULLINGER, B.A. Crown 8vo. 4*s*. 6*d*.

MYERS.—*St. Paul.*
A Poem. By F. W. H. MYERS. *Second Edition.* Extra fcap. 8vo. 2*s*. 6*d*.

NETTLESHIP.—*Essays on Robert Browning's Poetry.*
By JOHN T. NETTLESHIP. Extra fcap. 8vo. 6*s*. 6*d*.

New Landlord, The.
Translated from the Hungarian of MAURICE JOKAI by A. J. PATTERSON. Two vols. crown 8vo. 21*s*.

Northern Circuit.
Brief Notes of Travel in Sweden, Finland, and Russia. With a Frontispiece. Crown 8vo. 5*s*.

NORTON.—*The Lady of La Garaye.*
By the Hon. Mrs. NORTON. With Vignette and Frontispiece. *Sixth Edition.* Fcap. 8vo. 4*s*. 6*d*.

O'BRIEN.—*Works by* JAMES THOMAS O'BRIEN, D.D. *Bishop of Ossory.*

An Attempt to Explain and Establish the Doctrine of Justification by Faith only.
Third Edition. 8vo. 12*s.*

Charge delivered at the Visitation in 1863.
Second Edition. 8vo. 2*s.*

OLIPHANT.—*Agnes Hopetoun's Schools and Holidays.*
By Mrs. OLIPHANT. Royal 16mo. gilt leaves. 3*s.* 6*d.*

OLIVER.—*Lessons in Elementary Botany.*
With nearly 200 Illustrations. By DANIEL OLIVER, F.R.S.
F.L.S. 18mo. 4*s.* 6*d.*

OPPEN.—*French Reader,*
For the Use of Colleges and Schools. By EDWARD A. OPPEN.
Fcap. 8vo. 4*s.* 6*d.*

ORWELL.—*The Bishop's Walk and the Bishop's Times.*
Poems on the Days of Archbishop Leighton and the Scottish
Covenant. By ORWELL. Fcap. 8vo. 5*s.*

Our Year.
A Child's Book, in Prose and Verse. By the Author of "John
Halifax, Gentleman." Illustrated by CLARENCE DOBELL. Royal
16mo. 3*s.* 6*d.*

PALGRAVE.—*History of Normandy and of England.*
By Sir FRANCIS PALGRAVE. Completing the History to the
Death of William Rufus. Vols. I. to IV. 8vo. each 21*s.*

PALGRAVE.—*A Narrative · of a Year's Journey through Central and Eastern Arabia,* 1862-3.
By WILLIAM GIFFORD PALGRAVE (late of the Eighth Regiment
Bombay N.I.) *Fourth and Cheaper Edition.* With Map, Plans
and Portrait of Author, engraved on Steel by JEENS. Crown
8vo. 7*s.* 6*d.*

PALGRAVE.—*Works by* FRANCIS TURNER PALGRAVE, M.A.
late Fellow of Exeter College, Oxford.

The Five Days' Entertainments at Wentworth Grange.
Small 4to. 9*s.*

PALGRAVE.—*Essays on Art:*
  Mulready—Dyce—Holman Hunt—Herbert—Poetry, Prose, and Sensationalism in Art—Sculpture in England—The Albert Cross, &c. Extra fcap. 8vo. 6s.

Sonnets and Songs.
  By WILLIAM SHAKESPEARE. GEM EDITION. With Vignette Title by JEENS. 3s. 6d.

Original Hymns.
  Second Edition, enlarged. 18mo. 1s. 6d.

PALMER.—*The Book of Praise:*
  From the Best English Hymn Writers. Selected and arranged by SIR ROUNDELL PALMER. With Vignette by WOOLNER. 18mo. 4s. 6d. *Large Type Edition,* demy 8vo. 10s. 6d. morocco, 21s.

A Hymnal.
  Chiefly from the BOOK OF PRAISE. In various sizes.
  A.—In royal 32mo. cloth limp. 6d.
  B.—Small 18mo. larger type, cloth limp. 1s.
  C.—Same Edition, fine paper, cloth. 1s. 6d.
  An Edition with Music, Selected, Harmonized, and Composed by JOHN HULLAH. Square 18mo. 3s. 6d.

PARKINSON.—*Works by* S. PARKINSON, B.D.

A Treatise on Elementary Mechanics.
  For the Use of the Junior Classes at the University and the Higher Classes in Schools. With a Collection of Examples. *Third Edition, revised.* Crown 8vo. 9s. 6d.

A Treatise on Optics.
  Second Edition, revised. Crown 8vo. 10s. 6d.

PATMORE.—*Works by* COVENTRY PATMORE.

The Angel in the House.
  Book I. The Betrothal.—Book II. The Espousals.—Book III. Faithful for Ever. With Tamerton Church Tower. Two vols. fcap. 8vo. 12s.
  ** A New and Cheap Edition, in one vol. 18mo. beautifully printed on toned paper, price 2s. 6d.

The Victories of Love.
  Fcap. 8vo. 4s. 6d.

Phantasmagoria and other Poems.
  By LEWIS CARROLL.

PHEAR.—*Elementary Hydrostatics.*
  By J. B. PHEAR, M.A. *Third Edition.* Crown 8vo. 5s. 6d.

PHILLIMORE.—*Private Law among the Romans.*
From the Pandects. By JOHN GEORGE PHILLIMORE, Q.C.
8vo. 16s.

Philology.
The Journal of Sacred and Classical Philology. Four Vols. 8vo.
12s. 6d. each.
The Journal of Philology. New Series. Edited by W. G. CLARK,
M.A. JOHN E. B. MAYOR, M.A. and W. ALDIS WRIGHT, M.A.
No. I. 8vo. 4s. 6d. (Half-yearly.)

PLATO.—*The Republic of Plato.*
Translated into English, with Notes. By Two Fellows of Trinity
College, Cambridge (J. Ll. Davies, M.A. and D. J. Vaughan.
M.A.). With Vignette Portraits of Plato and Socrates engraved
by JEENS from an Antique Gem. (Golden Treasury Series.) *New
Edition*, 18mo. 4s. 6d.

Platonic Dialogues, The,
For English Readers. By the late W. WHEWELL, D.D. F.R.S.
Master of Trinity College, Cambridge. Vol. I. *Second Edition*,
containing *The Socratic Dialogues*, fcap. 8vo. 7s. 6d. ; Vol. II.
containing *The Anti-Sophist Dialogues*, 6s. 6d.; Vol. III. containing *The Republic*, 7s. 6d.

Plea for a New English Version of the Scriptures.
By a Licentiate of the Church of Scotland. 8vo. 6s.

POTTER.—*A Voice from the Church in Australia :*
Sermons preached in Melbourne. By the Rev. ROBERT POTTER
M.A. Extra fcap. 8vo. 4s. 6d.

Practitioner (The), a Monthly Journal of Therapeutics.
Edited by FRANCIS E. ANSTIE, M.D. and HENRY LAWSON
M.D. 8vo. Price 1s. 6d.

PRATT.—*Treatise on Attractions, La Place's Functions,
and the Figure of the Earth.*
By J. H. PRATT, M.A. *Third Edition*. Crown 8vo. 6s. 6d.

PRESCOTT.—*The Threefold Cord.*
Sermons preached before the University of Cambridge. By
J. E. PRESCOTT, B.D. Fcap. 8vo. 3s. 6d.

PROCTER.—*Works by* FRANCIS PROCTER, M.A.

A History of the Book of Common Prayer :
With a Rationale of its Offices. *Seventh Edition, revised and
enlarged*. Crown 8vo. 10s. 6d.

PROCTER AND G. F. MACLEAR, B.D.—*An Elementary History
of the Book of Common Prayer. New Edition.*
18mo. 2s. 6d.

Psalms of David chronologically arranged.
An Amended Version, with Historical Introductions and Explanatory Notes. By FOUR FRIENDS. Crown 8vo. 10s. 6d.

PUCKLE.—*An Elementary Treatise on Conic Sections and Algebraic Geometry, with numerous Examples and Hints for their Solution,*
Especially designed for the Use of Beginners. By G. HALE PUCKLE, M.A. Head Master of Windermere College. *Third Edition, enlarged.* Crown 8vo. 7s. 6d.

PULLEN.—*The Psalter and Canticles, Pointed for Chanting,*
With Marks of Expression, and a List of Appropriate Chants. By the Rev. HENRY PULLEN, M.A. 8vo. 5s.

RALEGH.—*The Life of Sir Walter Ralegh, based upon Contemporary Documents.*
By EDWARD EDWARDS. Together with his LETTERS, now first Collected. With Portrait. Two Vols. 8vo. 32s.

RAMSAY.—*The Catechiser's Manual;*
Or, the Church Catechism Illustrated and Explained, for the Use of Clergymen, Schoolmasters, and Teachers. By ARTHUR RAMSAY, M.A. *Second Edition.* 18mo. 1s. 6d.

RAWLINSON.—*Elementary Statics.*
By G. RAWLINSON, M.A. Edited by EDWARD STURGES, M.A. Crown 8vo. 4s. 6d.

Rays of Sunlight for Dark Days.
A Book of Selections for the Suffering. With a Preface by C. J. VAUGHAN, D.D. 18mo. *New Edition.* 3s. 6d. Morocco, old style, 7s. 6d.

Reform.—Essays on Reform.
By the Hon. G. C. BRODRICK, R. H. HUTTON, LORD HOUGHTON, A. V. DICEY, LESLIE STEPHEN, J. B. KINNEAR, B. CRACROFT, C. H. PEARSON, GOLDWIN SMITH, JAMES BRYCE, A. L. RUTSON, and Sir GEO. YOUNG. 8vo. 10s. 6d.

Questions for a Reformed Parliament.
By F. H. HILL, GODFREY LUSHINGTON, MEREDITH TOWNSEND, W. L. NEWMAN, C. S. PARKER, J. B. KINNEAR, G. HOOPER, F. HARRISON, Rev. J. E. T. ROGERS, J. M. LUDLOW, and LLOYD JONES. 8vo. 10s. 6d.

C

REYNOLDS.—*A System of Medicine. Vol. I.*

Edited by J. RUSSELL REYNOLDS, M.D. F.R.C.P. London. PART I. GENERAL DISEASES, or Affections of the Whole System. § I.—Those determined by agents operating from without, such as the exanthemata, malarial diseases, and their allies. § II.—Those determined by conditions existing within the body, such as Gout, Rheumatism, Rickets, &c. PART II. LOCAL DISEASES, or Affections of particular Systems. § I.— Diseases of the Skin. 8vo. 25s.

REYNOLDS.—*A System of Medicine. Vol. II.*

PART II. § I.—Diseases of the Nervous System. A. General Nervous Diseases. B. Partial Diseases of the Nervous System. 1. Diseases of the Head. 2. Diseases of the Spinal Column. 3. Diseases of the Nerves. § II.—Diseases of the Digestive System. A. Diseases of the Stomach. 8vo. 25s.

Notes of the Christian Life.

A Selection of Sermons by HENRY ROBERT REYNOLDS, B.A. President of Cheshunt College, and Fellow of University College, London. Crown 8vo. 7s. 6d.

REYNOLDS.—*Modern Methods of Elementary Geometry.*

By E. M. REYNOLDS, M.A. Mathematical Master in Clifton College. Crown 8vo. 3s. 6d.

Ridicula Rediviva.

Being old Nursery Rhymes. With Coloured Illustrations by J. E. ROGERS. 9s.

ROBERTS.—*Discussions on the Gospels.*

By the Rev. ALEXANDER ROBERTS, D.D. *Second Edition, revised and enlarged.* 8vo. 16s.

ROBERTSON.—*Pastoral Counsels.*

By the late JOHN ROBERTSON, D.D. of Glasgow Cathedral. New Edition. With Biographical Sketch by the Author of "Recreations of a Country Parson." Extra fcap. 8vo. 6s.

ROBINSON CRABB.—*Life and Reminiscences.* [In the Press.

ROBY.—*A Latin Grammar for the Higher Classes in Grammar Schools, based on the "Elementary Latin Grammar."*

By H. J. ROBY, M.A. [In the Press.

ROBY.—*Story of a Household, and other Poems.*

By MARY K. ROBY. Fcap. 8vo. 5s.

ROMANIS.—*Sermons preached at St. Mary's, Reading.*

By WILLIAM ROMANIS, M.A. *First Series.* Fcap. 8vo 6s Also, *Second Series.* 6s.

ROSCOE.—*Lessons in Elementary Chemistry, Inorganic and Organic.*
> By H. E. ROSCOE, F.R.S. *Eighth Thousand.* 18mo. *4s. 6d.*

ROSSETTI.—*Works by* CHRISTINA ROSSETTI.
Goblin Market, and other Poems.
> With Two Designs by D. G. ROSSETTI. *Second Edition.* Fcap. 8vo. *5s.*

The Prince's Progress, and other Poems.
> With Two Designs by D. G. ROSSETTI. Fcap. 8vo. *6s.*

ROSSETTI.—*Works by* WILLIAM MICHAEL ROSSETTI.
Dante's Comedy, The Hell.
> Translated into Literal Blank Verse. Fcap. 8vo. *5s.*

Fine Art, chiefly Contemporary.
> Crown 8vo. *10s. 6d.*

ROUTH.—*Treatise on Dynamics of Rigid Bodies.*
> With Numerous Examples. By E. J. ROUTH, M.A. *New Edition.* Crown 8vo. *14s.*

ROWSELL.—*Works by* T. J. ROWSELL, M.A.
The English Universities and the English Poor.
> Sermons preached before the University of Cambridge. Fcap. 8vo. *2s.*

Man's Labour and God's Harvest.
> Sermons preached before the University of Cambridge in Lent, 1861. Fcap. 8vo. *3s.*

RUFFINI.—*Vincenzo ; or, Sunken Rocks.*
> By JOHN RUFFINI. Three vols. crown 8vo. *31s. 6d.*

Ruth and her Friends.
> A Story for Girls. With a Frontispiece. *Fourth Edition.* Royal 16mo. *3s. 6d.*

SCOTT.—*Discourses.*
> By A. J. SCOTT, M.A. late Professor of Logic in Owens College, Manchester. Crown 8vo. *7s. 6d.*

couring of the White Horse.
> Or, the Long Vacation Ramble of a London Clerk. By the Author of "Tom Brown's School Days." Illustrated by DOYLE. *Eighth Thousand.* Imp. 16mo. *8s. 6d.*

SEATON.—*A Hand-Book of Vaccination.*
> By EDWARD C. SEATON, M.D. Medical Inspector to the Privy Council. Extra fcap. 8vo. *8s. 6d.*

SELKIRK.—*Guide to the Cricket Ground.*
>> By G. H. SELKIRK. With Woodcuts. Extra Fcap. 8vo. 3s. 6d.

SELWYN.—*The Work of Christ in the World.*
>> By G. A. SELWYN, D.D. Bishop of Lichfield. *Third Edition.* Crown 8vo. 2s.

SHAKESPEARE.—*The Works of William Shakespeare. Cambridge Edition.*
>> Edited by WM. GEORGE CLARK, M.A. and W. ALDIS WRIGHT, M.A. Nine Vols. 8vo. cloth. 4l. 14s. 6d.

Shakespeare's Tempest.
>> With Glossarial and Explanatory Notes. By the Rev. J. M. JEPHSON. 18mo. 1s. 6d.

SHAIRP.—*Kilmahoe, and other Poems.*
>> By J. CAMPBELL SHAIRP. Fcap. 8vo. 5s.

SHIRLEY.—*Elijah ; Four University Sermons.*
>> I. Samaria. II. Carmel. III. Kishon. IV. Horeb. By W.W SHIRLEY, D.D. Fcap. 8vo. 2s. 6d.

SIMPSON.—*An Epitome of the History of the Christian Church.*
>> By WILLIAM SIMPSON, M.A. *Fourth Edition.* Fcap. 8vo. 3s. 6d.

SMITH.—*Works by* ALEXANDER SMITH.

A Life Drama, and other Poems.
>> Fcap. 8vo. 2s. 6d.

City Poems.
>> Fcap. 8vo. 5s.

Edwin of Deira.
>> *Second Edition.* Fcap. 8vo. 5s.

SMITH.—*Poems by* CATHERINE BARNARD SMITH.
>> Crown 8vo. 5s.

SMITH.—*Works by* GOLDWIN SMITH.

A Letter to a Whig Member of the Southern Independence Association.
>> Extra fcap. 8vo. 2s.

Three English Statesmen ; Pym, Cromwell, and Pitt.
>> A Course of Lectures on the Political History of England. Extra fcap. 8vo. *New and Cheaper Edition.* 5s.

SMITH.— *Works by* BARNARD SMITH, M.A. *Rector of Glaston,
Rutland, &c.*

Arithmetic and Algebra.
Tenth Edition. Crown 8vo. 10*s.* 6*d.*

Arithmetic for the Use of Schools.
Ninth Edition. Crown 8vo. 4*s.* 6*d.*

A Key to the Arithmetic for Schools.
Fifth Edition. Crown 8vo. 8*s.* 6*d.*

Exercises in Arithmetic.
With Answers. Cr. 8vo. limp cloth, 2*s.* 6*d.* Or sold separately
as follows :—Part I. 1*s.* Part II. 1*s.* Answers, 6*d.*

School Class Book of Arithmetic.
18mo. 3*s.* Or sold separately, Parts I. and II. 10*d.* each.
Part III. 1*s.*

Keys to School Class Book of Arithmetic.
Complete in One Volume, 18mo. 6*s.* 6*d.* ; or Parts I. II. and III.
2*s.* 6*d.* each.

Shilling Book of Arithmetic for National and Elementary Schools.
18mo. cloth. Or separately, Part I. 2*d.* ; II. 3*d.* ; III. 7*d.*

Answers to the Shilling Book of Arithmetic.
18mo. 6*d.*

Key to the Shilling Book of Arithmetic.
18mo. 4*s.* 6*d.*

Examination Papers in Arithmetic.
In Four Parts. 18mo. 1*s.* 6*d.* With Answers, 1*s.* 9*d.*

Key to Examination Papers in Arithmetic.
18mo. 4*s.* 6*d.*

SMITH.—*Hymns of Christ and the Christian Life.*
By the Rev. WALTER C. SMITH, M.A. Fcap. 8vo. 6*s.*

SMITH.—*Obstacles to Missionary Success among the Heathen.*
The Maitland Prize Essay for 1867. By W. S. SMITH, M.A.
Fellow of Trinity College, Cambridge. Crown 8vo. 3*s.* 6*d.*

SMITH.—*A Treatise on Elementary Statics.*
By J. H. SMITH, M.A. Gonville and Caius College, Cambridge
Royal 8vo. 5*s.* 6*d.*

SMITH.—*A Treatise on Elementary Trigonometry.*
Royal 8vo. 5s.

A Treatise on Elementary Hydrostatics.
Royal 8vo. 4s. 6d.

SNOWBALL.—*The Elements of Plane and Spherical Trigonometry.*
By J. C. SNOWBALL, M.A. *Tenth Edition.* Crown 8vo. 7s. 6d.

Social Duties considered with Reference to the Organization of Effort in Works of Benevolence and Public Utility.
By a MAN OF BUSINESS. Fcap. 8vo. 4s. 6d.

SPENCER.—*Elements of Qualitative Chemical Analysis.*
By W. H. SPENCER, B.A. 4to. 10s. 6d.

Spring Songs.
By a WEST HIGHLANDER. With a Vignette Illustration by GOURLAY STEELE. Fcap. 8vo. 1s. 6d.

STEPHEN.—*General View of the Criminal Law of England.*
By J. FITZ-JAMES STEPHEN. 8vo. 18s.

STRATFORD DE REDCLIFFE.—*Shadows of the Past, in Verse.*
By VISCOUNT STRATFORD DE REDCLIFFE. Crown 8vo. 10s. 6d.

STRICKLAND.—*On Cottage Construction and Design.*
By C. W. STRICKLAND. With Specifications and Plans. Svo. 7s. 6d.

Sunday Library for Household Reading. Illustrated.
Monthly Parts, 1s. ; Quarterly Vols. 4s. Gilt edges, 4s. 6d.
Vol. I.—The Pupils of St. John the Divine, by the Author of "The Heir of Redclyffe."
Vol. II.—The Hermits, by PROFESSOR KINGSLEY.
Vol. III.—Seekers after God, by the Rev. F. W. FARRAR.
Vol. IV.—England's Antiphon, by GEORGE MACDONALD, LL.D.

SWAINSON.—*Works by* C. A. SWAINSON, D.D.

A Handbook to Butler's Analogy.
Crown 8vo. 1s. 6d.

The Creeds of the Church in their Relations to Holy Scripture and the Conscience of the Christian.
8vo. cloth. 9s.

The Authority of the New Testament,
And other Lectures, delivered before the University of Cambridge. 8vo. cloth. 12s.

TACITUS.—*The History of Tacitus translated into English.*
By A. J. CHURCH, M.A. and W. J. BRODRIBB, M.A. With a Map and Notes. 8vo. 10*s.* 6*d.*

The Agricola and Germany.
By the same Translators. With Map and Notes. Fcap. 8vo. 2*s.* 6*d.*

TAIT AND STEELE.—*A Treatise on Dynamics.*
With numerous Examples. By P. G. TAIT and W. J. STEELE. *Second Edition.* Crown 8vo. 10*s.* 6*d.*

TAYLOR.—*Words and Places;*
Or, Etymological Illustrations of History, Ethnology, and Geography. By the Rev. ISAAC TAYLOR. *Second Edition.* Crown 8vo. 12*s.* 6*d.*

TAYLOR.—*The Restoration of Belief.*
New and Revised Edition. By ISAAC TAYLOR, Esq. Crown 8vo. 8*s.* 6*d.*

TAYLOR (C.).—*Geometrical Conics.*
By C. TAYLOR, B.A. Crown 8vo. 7*s.* 6*d.*

TEBAY.—*Elementary Mensuration for Schools,*
With numerous Examples. By SEPTIMUS TEBAY, B.A. Head Master of Queen Elizabeth's Grammar School, Rivington. Extra fcap. 8vo. 3*s.* 6*d.*

TEMPLE.—*Sermons preached in the Chapel of Rugby School.*
By F. TEMPLE, D.D. Head Master. *New and Cheaper Edition.* Crown 8vo. 7*s.* 6*d.*

THORPE.—*Diplomatarium Anglicum Ævi Saxonici.*
A Collection of English Charters, from the Reign of King Æthelberht of Kent, A.D. DC.V. to that of William the Conqueror. With a Translation of the Anglo-Saxon. By BENJAMIN THORPE, Member of the Royal Academy of Sciences, Munich. 8vo. cloth. 21*s.*

THRING.—*Works by EDWARD THRING, M.A. Head Master of Uppingham.*

A Construing Book.
Fcap. 8vo. 2*s.* 6*d.*

A Latin Gradual.
A First Latin Construing Book for Beginners. 18mo. 2*s.* 6*d.*

The Elements of Grammar taught in English.
Fourth Edition. 18mo. 2*s.*

THRING.—*The Child's Grammar.*
A New Edition. 18mo. 1s.

Sermons delivered at Uppingham School.
Crown 8vo. 5s.

School Songs.
With the Music arranged for Four Voices. Edited by the Rev.
EDWARD THRING, M.A. and H. RICCIUS. Small folio. 7s. 6d.

Education and School.
Second Edition. Crown 8vo. 6s.

A Manual of Mood Constructions.
Extra fcap. 8vo. 1s. 6d.

THRUPP.—*Works by the Rev. J. F. THRUPP.*

The Song of Songs.
A New Translation, with a Commentary and an Introduction.
Crown 8vo. 7s. 6d.

Introduction to the Study and Use of the Psalms.
Two Vols. 8vo. 21s.

Psalms and Hymns for Public Worship.
Selected and Edited by the Rev. J. F. THRUPP, M.A. 18mo.
2s. Common paper, 1s. 4d.

The Burden of Human Sin as borne by Christ.
Three Sermons preached before the University of Cambridge in
Lent, 1865. Crown 8vo. 3s. 6d.

THUCYDIDES.—*The Sicilian Expedition:*
Being Books VI. and VII. of Thucydides, with Notes. By the
Rev. PERCIVAL FROST, M.A. Fcap. 8vo. 5s.

TOCQUEVILLE.—*Memoir, Letters, and Remains of Alexis de
Tocqueville.*
Translated from the French by the Translator of "Napoleon's
Correspondence with King Joseph." With numerous Additions.
Two vols. Crown 8vo. 21s.

TODD.—*The Books of the Vaudois.*
The Waldensian Manuscripts preserved in the Library of Trinity
College, Dublin, with an Appendix by JAMES HENTHORN TODD,
D.D. Crown 8vo. cloth. 6s.

TODHUNTER.—*Works by* ISAAC TODHUNTER, M.A. F.R.S.

Euclid for Colleges and Schools.
New Edition.   18mo.   3s. 6d.

Algebra for Beginners.
With numerous Examples.   *New Edition.*   18mo.   2s. 6d.

Key to Algebra for Beginners.
Crown 8vo.   6s. 6d.

Mechanics for Beginners.
With numerous Examples.   18mo.   4s. 6d.

Trigonometry for Beginners.
With numerous Examples.   18mo.   2s. 6d.

A Treatise on the Differential Calculus.
With numerous Examples.   *Fourth Edition.*   Crown 8vo.   10s. 6d.

A Treatise on the Integral Calculus.
With numerous Examples.   *Third Edition.*   Crown 8vo.   10s. 6d.

A Treatise on Analytical Statics.
Third Edition.   Crown 8vo.   10s. 6d.

A Treatise on Conic Sections.
Fourth Edition.   Crown 8vo.   7s. 6d.

Algebra for the Use of Colleges and Schools.
Fourth Edition.   Crown 8vo.   7s. 6d.

Plane Trigonometry for Colleges and Schools.
Third Edition.   Crown 8vo.   5s.

A Treatise on Spherical Trigonometry for the Use of Colleges and Schools.
Second Edition.   Crown 8vo.   4s. 6d.

Critical History of the Progress of the Calculus of Variations during the Nineteenth Century.
8vo.   12s.

Examples of Analytical Geometry of Three Dimensions.
Second Edition.   Crown 8vo.   4s.

A Treatise on the Theory of Equations.
Second Edition.   Crown 8vo.   7s. 6d.

Mathematical Theory of Probability.
8vo.   18s.

Tom Brown's School Days.
> By an OLD BOY. Fcap. 8vo. *5s.*
> Golden Treasury Edition, 4s. 6d.
> PEOPLE'S EDITION, 2s.
> Illustrated Edition.

Tom Brown at Oxford.
> By the Author of "Tom Brown's School Days." *New Edition.*
> Crown 8vo. 6s.

Tracts for Priests and People. (*By various Writers.*)
> THE FIRST SERIES, Crown 8vo. 8s.
> THE SECOND SERIES, Crown 8vo. 8s.
> The whole Series of Fifteen Tracts may be had separately, price
> One Shilling each.

TRENCH.—*Works by* R. CHENEVIX TRENCH, D.D. *Archbishop
of Dublin.*

Notes on the Parables of Our Lord.
> *Tenth Edition.* 8vo. 12s.

Notes on the Miracles of Our Lord.
> *Eighth Edition.* 8vo. 12s.

Synonyms of the New Testament.
> *New Edition.* One vol. 8vo. cloth. 10s. 6d.

On the Study of Words.
> *Twelfth Edition.* Fcap. 8vo. 4s.

English Past and Present.
> *Sixth Edition.* Fcap. 8vo. 4s. 6d.

Proverbs and their Lessons.
> *Fifth Edition.* Fcap. 8vo. 3s.

*Select Glossary of English Words used formerly in
Senses different from the present.*
> *Third Edition.* Fcap. 8vo. 4s.

On some Deficiencies in our English Dictionaries.
> *Second Edition.* 8vo. 3s.

Sermons preached in Westminster Abbey.
> *Second Edition.* 8vo. 10s. 6d.

*The Fitness of Holy Scripture for Unfolding the
Spiritual Life of Man :*
> Christ the Desire of all Nations; or, the Unconscious Prophecies
> of Heathendom. Hulsean Lectures. Fcap. 8vo. *Fourth Edition.*
> *5s.*

TRENCH (R. CHENEVIX)—*On the Authorized Version of the New Testament.*
>Second Edition. 8vo. 7s.

Justin Martyr, and other Poems.
>Fifth Edition. Fcap. 8vo. 6s.

Gustavus Adolphus.—Social Aspects of the Thirty Years' War.
>Fcap. 8vo. 2s. 6d.

Poems.
>Collected and arranged anew. Fcap. 8vo. 7s. 6d.

Poems from Eastern Sources, Genoveva, and other Poems.
>Second Edition. Fcap. 8vo. 5s. 6d.

Elegiac Poems.
>Third Edition. Fcap. 8vo. 2s. 6d.

Calderon's Life's a Dream :
>The Great Theatre of the World. With an Essay on his Life and Genius. Fcap. 8vo. 4s. 6d.

Remains of the late Mrs. Richard Trench.
>Being Selections from her Journals, Letters, and other Papers. *New and Cheaper Issue.* With Portrait. 8vo. 6s.

Commentary on the Epistles to the Seven Churches in Asia.
>Third Edition, revised. 8vo. 8s. 6d.

Sacred Latin Poetry.
>Chiefly Lyrical. Selected and arranged for Use. *Second Edition.* Corrected and Improved. Fcap. 8vo. 7s.

Studies in the Gospels.
>Second Edition. 8vo. 10s. 6d.

Shipwrecks of Faith :
>Three Sermons preached before the University of Cambridge in May, 1867. Fcap. 8vo. 2s. 6d.

A Household Book of English Poetry.
>Selected and Arranged with Notes. By the ARCHBISHOP OF DUBLIN. Extra fcap. 8vo. 5s. 6d.

TRENCH (REV. FRANCIS).—*Brief Notes on the Greek of the New Testament (for English Readers).*
>Crown 8vo. cloth. 6s.

TREVELYAN.—*Works by* G. O. TREVELYAN, M.P.

The Competition Wallah.
New Edition. Crown 8vo. 6s.

Cawnpore,
Illustrated with Plan. Second Edition. Crown 8vo. 6s.

TUDOR.—*The Decalogue viewed as the Christian's Law.*
With Special Reference to the Questions and Wants of the Times.
By the Rev. RICH. TUDOR, B.A. Crown 8vo. 10s. 6d.

TULLOCH.—*The Christ of the Gospels and the Christ of*
Modern Criticism.
Lectures on M. RENAN'S "Vie de Jésus." By JOHN TULLOCH,
D.D. Principal of the College of St. Mary, in the University of
St. Andrew. Extra fcap. 8vo. 4s. 6d.

TURNER.—*Sonnets.*
By the Rev. CHARLES TENNYSON TURNER. Dedicated to his
Brother, the Poet Laureate. Fcap. 8vo. 4s. 6d.

Small Tableaux.
By the Rev. C. TURNER. Fcap. 8vo. 4s. 6d.

TYRWHITT.—*The Schooling of Life.*
By R. ST. JOHN TYRWHITT, M.A. Vicar of St. Mary Magdalen,
Oxford. Fcap. 8vo. 3s. 6d.

Vacation Tourists ;
And Notes of Travel in 1861. Edited by F. GALTON, F.R.S.
With Ten Maps illustrating the Routes. 8vo. 14s.

Vacation Tourists ;
And Notes of Travel in 1862 and 1863. Edited by FRANCIS
GALTON, F.R.S. 8vo. 16s.

VAUGHAN.—*Works by* CHARLES J. VAUGHAN, D.D. *Vicar*
of Doncaster.

Notes for Lectures on Confirmation.
With suitable Prayers. Sixth Edition. Fcap. 8vo. 1s. 6d.

Lectures on the Epistle to the Philippians.
Second Edition. Crown 8vo. 7s. 6d.

Lectures on the Revelation of St. John.
Second Edition. Two vols. crown 8vo. 15s.

VAUGHAN (CHARLES J.).—*Epiphany, Lent, and Easter.*
A Selection of Expository Sermons. ***Third Edition.*** Crown
8vo. 10s. 6d.

The Book and the Life,
And other Sermons, preached before the University of Cambridge. *New Edition.* Fcap. 8vo. 4s. 6d.

Memorials of Harrow Sundays.
A Selection of Sermons preached in Harrow School Chapel.
With a View of the Chapel. ***Fourth Edition.*** Crown 8vo.
10s. 6d.

St. Paul's Epistle to the Romans.
The Greek Text with English Notes. Crown 8vo. 5s. *New
Edition in the Press.*

*Twelve Discourses on Subjects connected with the Liturgy
and Worship of the Church of England.*
Fcap. 8vo. 6s.

Lessons of Life and Godliness.
A Selection of Sermons preached in the Parish Church of Doncaster. *Third Edition.* Fcap. 8vo. 4s. 6d.

Words from the Gospels.
A Second Selection of Sermons preached in the Parish Church of
Doncaster. *Second Edition.* Fcap. 8vo. 4s. 6d.

The Epistles of St. Paul.
For English Readers. Part I. containing the First Epistle to
the Thessalonians. *Second Edition.* 8vo. 1s. 6d. Each Epistle
will be published separately.

The Church of the First Days.
Series I. The Church of Jerusalem. *Second Edition.*
  ,, II. The Church of the Gentiles. *Second Edition.*
  ,, III. The Church of the World. *Second Edition.*
Fcap. 8vo. cloth. 4s. 6d. each.

Life's Work and God's Discipline.
Three Sermons. Fcap. 8vo. cloth. 2s. 6d.

The Wholesome Words of Jesus Christ.
Four Sermons preached before the University of Cambridge in
November, 1866. Fcap. 8vo. cloth. 3s. 6d. *New Edition in
the Press.*

Foes of Faith.
Sermons preached before the University of Cambridge in
November, 1868.

VAUGHAN.—*Works by* DAVID J. VAUGHAN, M.A. *Vicar of St. Martin's, Leicester.*

Sermons preached in St. John's Church, Leicester,
During the Years 1855 and 1856. Crown 8vo. **5s. 6d.**

Sermons on the Resurrection.
With a Preface. Fcap. 8vo. **3s.**

Three Sermons on the Atonement.
1s. 6d.

Sermons on Sacrifice and Propitiation.
2s. 6d.

Christian Evidences and the Bible.
New Edition. Revised and enlarged. Fcap. 8vo. cloth. **5s. 6d.**

VAUGHAN.—*Memoir of Robert A. Vaughan,*
Author of "Hours with the Mystics." By ROBERT VAUGHAN, D.D. *Second Edition.* Revised and enlarged. Extra fcap. 8vo. **5s.**

VENN.—*The Logic of Chance.*
An Essay on the Foundations and Province of the Theory of Probability, with special reference to its application to Moral and Social Science. By the Rev. J. VENN, M.A. Fcap. 8vo. **7s. 6d.**

Village Sermons.
By a NORTHAMPTONSHIRE RECTOR. With a Preface on the Inspiration of Holy Scripture. Crown 8vo. **6s.**

Vittoria Colonna.—Life and Poems.
By MRS. HENRY ROSCOE. Crown 8vo. **9s.**

Volunteer's Scrap Book.
By the Author of "The Cambridge Scrap Book." Crown 4to. **7s. 6d.**

WAGNER.—*Memoir of the Rev. George Wagner,*
late of St. Stephen's, Brighton. By J. N. SIMPKINSON, M.A. *Third and Cheaper Edition.* **5s.**

WALLACE.—*The Malay Archipelago: The Home of the Orang Utan and the Bird of Paradise.*
A Narrative of Travel. With Studies of Man and Nature. By ALFRED RUSSEL WALLACE. With Maps and Illustrations.

WARREN.—*An Essay on Greek Federal Coinage.*
By the Hon. J. LEICESTER WARREN, M.A. 8vo. 2*s.* 6*d.*

WEBSTER.—*Works by* AUGUSTA WEBSTER.

Dramatic Studies.
Extra fcap. 8vo. 5*s.*

A Woman Sold,.
And other Poems. Crown 8vo. 7*s.* 6*d.*

Prometheus Bound, of Æschylus,
Literally Translated into English Verse. Extra fcap. 8vo. 3*s.* 6*d.*

Medea of Euripides,
Literally Translated into English Verse. Extra fcap. 8vo. 3*s.* 6*d.*

WESTCOTT.—*Works by* BROOKE FOSS WESTCOTT. B.D.
Examining Chaplain to the Bishop of Peterborough.

A General Survey of the History of the Canon of the New Testament during the First Four Centuries.
Second Edition, revised. Crown 8vo. 10*s.* 6*d.*

·Characteristics of the Gospel Miracles.
Sermons preached before the University of Cambridge. *With Notes.* Crown 8vo. 4*s.* 6*d.*

Introduction to the Study of the Four Gospels.
Third Edition. Crown 8vo. 10*s.* 6*d.*

The Gospel of the Resurrection.
Thoughts on its Relation to Reason and History. *New Edition.* Fcap. 8vo. 4*s.* 6*d.*

The Bible in the Church.
A Popular Account of the Collection and Reception of the Holy Scriptures in the Christian Churches. *Second Edition.* 18mo. 4*s.* 6*d.*

History of the English Bible.
Crown 8vo. 10*s.* 6*d.*

Westminster Plays.
Lusus Alteri Westmonasterienses, Sive Prologi et Epilogi ad Fabulas in Sti Petri Collegio : actas qui Exstabant collecti et justa quoad licuit annorum serie ordinati, quibus accedit Declamationum quæ vocantur et Epigrammatum Delectus. Curantibus J. MURE, A.M., H. BULL, A.M., C. B. SCOTT, B.D. 8vo. 12*s.* 6*d.*

IDEM.—Pars Secunda, 1820—1865. Quibus accedit Epigrammatum Delectus. 8vo. 15*s.*

WILSON.—*Works by* GEORGE WILSON, M.D.
Counsels of an Invalid.
Letters on Religious Subjects. With Vignette Portrait. Fcap. 8vo. 4s. 6d.

Religio Chemici.
With a Vignette beautifully engraved after a Design by Sir NOEL PATON. Crown 8vo. 8s. 6d.

WILSON (GEORGE).—*The Five Gateways of Knowledge.*
New Edition. Fcap. 8vo. 2s. 6d. Or in Paper Covers, 1s.

The Progress of the Telegraph.
Fcap. 8vo. 1s.

WILSON.—*An English, Hebrew, and Chaldee Lexicon and Concordance.*
By WILLIAM WILSON, D.D. Canon of Winchester. *Second Edition.* 4to. 25s.

WILSON.—*Memoir of George Wilson, M.D. F.R.S.E.*
Regius Professor of Technology in the University of Edinburgh. By HIS SISTER. *New Edition.* Crown 8vo. 6s.

WILSON.—*Works by* DANIEL WILSON, L.L.D.
Prehistoric Annals of Scotland.
New Edition. With numerous Illustrations. Two Vols. demy 8vo. 36s.

Prehistoric Man.
New Edition. Revised and partly re-written, with numerous Illustrations. One vol. 8vo. 21s.

WILSON.—*A Treatise on Dynamics.*
By W. P. WILSON, M.A. 8vo. 9s. 6d.

WILSON.—*Elementary Geometry.*
PART I.—Angles, Triangles, Parallels, and Equivalent Figures, with the application to Problems. By J. M. WILSON, M.A. Fellow of St. John's College, Cambridge, and Mathematical Master at Rugby. Extra fcap. 8vo. 2s. 6d.

WINSLOW.—*Force and Nature. Attraction and Repulsion.*
The Radical Principles of Energy graphically discussed in their Relations to Physical and Morphological Development. By C. F. WINSLOW, M.D. 8vo. [In the press.

WOLLASTON.—*Lyra Devoniensis.*
By T. V. WOLLASTON, M.A. Fcap. 8vo. 3s. 6d.

WOLSTENHOLME.—*A Book of Mathematical Problems.*
Crown 8vo. 8s. 6d.

WOODFORD.—*Christian Sanctity.*
By JAMES RUSSELL WOODFORD, M.A. Fcap. 8vo. cloth. 3s.

WOODWARD.—*Works by the Rev.* HENRY WOODWARD, *edited by his Son,* THOMAS WOODWARD, M.A. *Dean of Down.*

Essays, Thoughts and Reflections, and Letters.
Fifth Edition. Crown 8vo. 10s. 6d.

The Shunammite.
Second Edition. Crown 8vo. 10s. 6d.

Sermons.
Fifth Edition. Crown 8vo. 10s. 6d.

WOOLLEY.—*Lectures delivered in Australia.*
By the late JOHN WOOLLEY, D.C.L. Crown 8vo. 8s. 6d.

WOOLNER.—*My Beautiful Lady.*
By THOMAS WOOLNER. With a Vignette by ARTHUR HUGHES.
Third Edition. Fcap. 8vo. 5s.

Words from the Poets.
Selected by the Editor of " Rays of Sunlight." With a Vignette
and Frontispiece. 18mo. Extra cloth gilt. 2s. 6d. *Cheaper
Edition,* 18mo. limp. 1s.

Worship (The) of God and Fellowship among Men.
Sermons on Public Worship. By PROFESSOR MAURICE, and
Others. Fcap. 8vo. 3s. 6d.

WORSLEY.—*Christian Drift of Cambridge Work.*
Eight Lectures. By T. WORSLEY, D.D. Master of Downing
College, Cambridge. Crown 8vo. cloth. 6s.

WRIGHT.—*Works by* J. WRIGHT, M.A.

Hellenica;
Or, a History of Greece in Greek, as related by Diodorus
and Thucydides, being a First Greek Reading Book, with
Explanatory Notes Critical and Historical. *Third Edition,*
WITH A VOCABULARY. 12mo. 3s. 6d.

D

The Seven Kings of Rome.

An Easy Narrative, abridged from the First Book of Livy by the omission of difficult passages, being a First Latin Reading Book, with Grammatical Notes. Fcap. 8vo. *3s.*

A Vocabulary and Exercises on the "Seven Kings of Rome."

Fcap. 8vo. *2s. 6d.*

** The Vocabulary and Exercises may also be had bound up with "The Seven Kings of Rome." Price *5s.*

A Help to Latin Grammar;

Or, the Form and Use of Words in Latin, with Progressive Exercises. Crown 8vo. *4s. 6d.*

David, King of Israel.

Readings for the Young. With Six Illustrations. Royal 16mo. cloth, gilt. *3s. 6d.*

YOUMANS.—*Modern Culture,*

Its True Aims and Requirements. A Series of Addresses and Arguments on the Claims of Scientific Education. Edited by EDWARD L. YOUMANS, M.D. Crown 8vo. *8s. 6d.*

𝔚𝔬𝔯𝔨𝔰 𝔟𝔶 𝔱𝔥𝔢 𝔄𝔲𝔱𝔥𝔬𝔯 𝔬𝔣

"THE HEIR OF REDCLYFFE."

The Prince and the Page. A Book for the Young. 18mo. **3s. 6d.**

A Book of Golden Deeds. 18mo. **4s. 6d.** Cheap Edition, 1s.

History of Christian Names. Two. Vols. Crown 8vo. **1l. 1s.**

The Heir of Redclyffe. Seventeenth Edition. With Illustrations.
Crown 8vo. 6s.

Dynevor Terrace. Third Edition. Crown 8vo. **6s.**

The Daisy Chain. Ninth Edition. With Illustrations. Crown 8vo. 6s.

The Trial: More Links of the Daisy Chain. Fourth Edition. With
Illustrations. Crown 8vo. 6s.

Heartsease. Tenth Edition. With Illustrations. Crown 8vo. 6s.

Hopes and Fears. Third Edition. Crown 8vo. **6s.**

The Young Stepmother. Second Edition. Crown 8vo. **6s.**

The Lances of Lynwood. With Coloured Illustrations. *Second Edition.*
Extra fcap. cloth. 4s. 6d.

The Little Duke. New Edition. 18mo. cloth. **3s. 6d.**

Clever Woman of the Family. Crown 8vo. **6s.**

Danvers Papers; an Invention. Crown 8vo. **4s. 6d.**

Dove in the Eagle's Nest. Two vols. Crown 8vo. **12s.**

Cameos from English History. From Rollo to Edward II. Extra
fcap. 8vo. 5s.

Book of Worthies. [In the Press.

ELEMENTARY SCHOOL CLASS BOOKS.

The Volumes of this Series of ELEMENTARY SCHOOL CLASS BOOKS are handsomely printed in a form that, it is hoped, will assist the young Student as much as clearness of type and distinctness of arrangement can effect. They are published at a moderate price, to insure an extensive sale in the Schools of the United Kingdom and the Colonies.

Euclid for Colleges and Schools.
By I. TODHUNTER, M.A. F.R.S. 18mo. 3s. 6d.

Algebra for Beginners.
By I. TODHUNTER, M.A. F.R.S. 18mo. 2s. 6d.

Key to Algebra for Beginners.
Crown 8vo. 6s. 6d.

The School Class Book of Arithmetic.
By BARNARD SMITH, M.A. Parts I. and II. 18mo. limp cloth, price 10d. each. Part III. 1s. ; or Three Parts in one Volume, price 3s.
KEY TO CLASS BOOK OF ARITHMETIC.
Complete, 18mo. cloth, price 6s. 6d. Or separately, Parts I. II. & III. 2s. 6d. each.

Mythology for Latin Versification.
A Brief Sketch of the Fables of the Ancients, prepared to be rendered into Latin Verse for Schools. By F. HODGSON, B.D. *New Edition.* Revised by F. C. HODGSON, M.A. Fellow of King's College, Cambridge. 18mo. 3s.

A Latin Gradual for Beginners.
A First Latin Construing Book. By EDWARD THRING, M.A. 18mo. 2s. 6d.

Shakespeare's Tempest.
The Text taken from "The Cambridge Shakespeare." With Glossarial and Explanatory Notes. By the Rev. J. M. JEPHSON. 18mo. cloth limp. 1s. 6d.

Lessons in Elementary Botany.
The Part on Systematic Botany based upon Material left in Manuscript by the late Professor HENSLOW. With nearly Two Hundred Illustrations. By DANIEL OLIVER, F.R.S. F.L.S. 18mo. cloth. 4s. 6d.

Lessons in Elementary Physiology.
With numerous Illustrations. By T. H. HUXLEY, F.R.S. Professor o Natural History in the Government School of Mines. 18mo. 4s. 6d.

Popular Astronomy.
A Series of Lectures delivered at Ipswich. By GEORGE BIDDELL AIRY, Astronomer Royal. 18mo. cloth. 4s. 6d.

Lessons in Elementary Chemistry.
By HENRY ROSCOE, F.R.S. Professor of Chemistry in Owens College, Manchester. With numerous Illustrations. 18mo. cloth. 4s. 6d.

An Elementary History of the Book of Common Prayer.
By FRANCIS PROCTER, M.A. 18mo. 2s. 6d.

Algebraical Exercises.
Progressively arranged by Rev. C. A. JONES, M.A. and C. H. CHEYNE, M.A. Mathematical Masters in Westminster School. 18mo. cloth. 2s. 6d.

The Bible in the Church.
A Popular Account of the Collection and Reception of the Holy Scriptures in the Christian Churches. By BROOKE FOSS WESTCOTT, B.D. 18mo. 4s. 6d.

The Bible Word Book.
A Glossary of Old English Bible Words. By J. EASTWOOD, M.A. and W. ALDIS WRIGHT, M.A. 18mo. 5s. 6d.

MACMILLAN AND CO. LONDON.